WHAT OTHERS ARE SAYING ABOUT STEVE STIRLING AND *THE CRUTCH OF SUCCESS*...

Do you believe God can use you to change the world? Or do you think you're not gifted enough, exceptional enough, or good enough? Meet Steve Stirling. Crippled by polio when he was just a baby and abandoned at a Korean orphanage when he was six, Steve was an unlikely candidate to change the world. But when you read the story of how God has used this humble man to impact the lives of hundreds of thousands of children all across the globe, you'll believe that God can use you too. Prepare to be amazed at what God can do with just one person's obedience.

—*Richard Stearns*
President Emeritus, World Vision US
Author, *The Hole in Our Gospel*

The Crutch of Success is a wonderful story of Steve and the life the Lord gave him. We have seen him, his lovely wife, and their two talented children at various times over the years. It is thrilling to know that he is the CEO of MAP, which has helped us back when we needed them. I am sure anyone who reads this book will be sincerely touched by the way the Lord has led Steve over the years.

—*Molly Holt*
Chairperson, Holt Children's Services (Holt Korea)

Steve's story is one of incredible resilience and the work of MAP International inspires many to join the global movement to bring critical medicines to those in need.

—*Jimmy Carter*
39th President of the United States

We hear that the purpose of life is a life of purpose. It seems remote as a saying until you meet a person with a purpose-driven life. Steve Stirling is such a person. To see him shrug off disabilities, as if they didn't exist, and then focus on preventing others from suffering from disabilities of all kinds, is a lesson for all seeking purpose in their own lives. As the head of MAP, Steve is daily involved in providing medicines and medical supplies to health workers around the world. These are daily redemptive acts of a person who lives a life of gratitude. This inspirational book describes how he has achieved a positive attitude, despite abandonment and disabilities that could have left a lesser person bitter and unproductive.

—*William H. Foege,* MD, MPH
Emeritus Presidential Distinguished Professor of International Health
Rollins School of Public Health, Emory University
Gates Fellow, The Bill and Melinda Gates Foundation

Steve Stirling is a remarkable success story, a story that would be hard to believe if it weren't true. *The Crutch of Success* tells his story well. It is an inspiring journey of a polio-stricken child in a small Korean orphanage to success in business and success in life.

—*Andrew J. Young Jr.*
Former U.S. Ambassador to the United Nations
Civil Rights Leader

Steve Stirling is a winner! Being with him in the Agalta Valley region of Honduras when MAP International delivered their five billionth donation in medicines was an amazing moment. The health and overall well-being of not only this Honduran community, but also other communities worldwide, would not be possible without Steve's dedication to his work. His inspiring life story is about the journey it takes to make triumphs out of obstacles and turn losses into wins.

—*Vince Dooley*
College Football Hall of Fame Inductee
Former Coach, University of Georgia

Steve is an Asian hero and role model of challenge. I have known him for twenty years. By faith in God, he has overcome his orphan life with a disabled body by challenging all of his obstacles in his difficult life journey. His life is a living testimony today. Also, his leadership at MAP is outstanding and making a difference all over the world.

—*Rev. Byeongho Choi*
Moderator-Elect, National Caucus of Korean Presbyterian Church
Senior Pastor, Bethany Presbyterian Church

Rotary International has been on a journey since the early 1980s to eradicate polio. There is not a more dedicated Rotarian who represents that journey as well as Steve Stirling. It is time for his story to be immortalized in writing, and all who read it will be motivated to reach beyond the barriers they encounter in their lives. It is a terrific story that will inspire us all.

—*John Hewko*
Secretary-General, Rotary International

Having known Steve personally and professionally for over nineteen years, I can attest to his courage, determination, sincerity, and faith. His story is one which inspires and shows his God-given purpose to serve. We witness his servant leadership at MAP International daily.

—*Jim Barfoot*

Chair, MAP International

THE CRUTCH OF SUCCESS

THE CRUTCH OF SUCCESS

From Polio to Purpose, Bringing Health & Hope to the World

STEVE STIRLING

WHITAKER HOUSE

The Crutch of Success
From Polio to Purpose, Bringing Health & Hope to the World

MAP International
4700 Glynco Parkway
Brunswick, GA 31525
map@map.org

ISBN: 978-1-64123-325-5 • eBook ISBN: 978-1-64123-326-2
Printed in the United States of America

Whitaker House
1030 Hunt Valley Circle • New Kensington, PA 15068
www.whitakerhouse.com

Library of Congress Cataloging-in-Publication Data
Names: Stirling, Steve, 1955- author.
Title: The crutch of success : from polio to purpose, bringing health & hope to the world / Steve Stirling.
Description: New Kensington, PA : Whitaker House, 2019. | Includes bibliographical references. | Summary: "The story of a polio survivor who was abandoned by his father in a Korean orphanage, adopted by an American couple, and gave up a corporate business career to bring medicines and health care to the world's poor"— Provided by publisher.
Identifiers: LCCN 2019022583 (print) | LCCN 2019022584 (ebook) | ISBN 9781641233255 (trade paperback) | ISBN 9781641233262 (ebook)
Subjects: LCSH: Stirling, Steve, 1955- | MAP International (Organization)—Officials and employees—Biography. | Poliomyelitis—Patients—United States—Biography. | Orphans—Korea (South)—Biography. | Poor—Medical care—Biography. | Faith-based human services—Developing countries.
Classification: LCC RC181.U5 S75 2019 (print) | LCC RC181.U5 (ebook) | DDC 616.8/350092 [B]—dc23
LC record available at https://lccn.loc.gov/2019022583
LC ebook record available at https://lccn.loc.gov/2019022584

1 2 3 4 5 6 7 8 9 10 11 W 26 25 24 23 22 21 20 19

DEDICATION

To my parents: the ones who gave birth to me, and the ones who gave me life through adoption.

To my wife, Sook Hee, for taking a chance on me, believing in me, and loving me.

To my children, Richard and Racheal, whom I love.

To my childhood friend, Song Kyung Soo, who opened my eyes to see how to live for Christ.

And to my friends, who have touched my life journey, enabling me to become who I am today.

For we are His workmanship,
created in Christ Jesus for good works,
which God prepared beforehand that we should walk in them.
—Ephesians 2:10

CONTENTS

FOREWORD

Before I read a book, I ask two basic questions: Does the author possess a level of credibility? And does he or she have something meaningful to say? Author and MAP International CEO, Steve Stirling, delivers on both counts. His book, *The Crutch of Success: From Polio to Purpose, Bringing Health & Hope to the World,* will challenge you to play your part in changing the world.

Steve is a living reminder that where you start in life doesn't have to dictate where you end. Through perseverance and faith, he overcame polio and an orphaned childhood to lead one of the largest international relief charities in the world. Convoy of Hope, the organization I founded, has partnered with MAP International to respond to natural and human-made disasters around the world. Countless lives have been rescued by delivering medicine and emergency supplies to children and families in need. It is a privilege to partner with an organization that pursues excellence with passion and urgency. When Steve speaks on global health and world crises, we have good reason to listen.

The Crutch of Success will increase your faith and help you discover your mission in life. If you've ever been told you aren't good enough, smart enough, or strong enough, this book will inspire you to believe, that with God's help, anything is possible. He will minimize your weaknesses and maximize your strengths. He longs to help the hurting and heal the sick. He just needs people like you to believe you can make the world a better place.

—*Hal Donaldson*
Founder and CEO, Convoy of Hope

PROLOGUE

"Wait right here, Son," said my father, sounding choked up. "If you cry, they will come and get you."

He had been carrying me in his arms, and now he leaned over to place me on the ground in a sitting position with my useless legs splayed out. He was wearing yesterday's white shirt. Looking up, I could see that his dress trousers, normally creased and cuffed, were wrinkled and dusty.

I was confused, but I trusted my *abba* (dad). Korea was not an easy place to live only three years after the end of the Korean War, but I knew nothing about that. Although polio had left me unable to walk at age one, my family had cared for me well. I was now a cheerful and energetic six-year-old.

Today was unusual in every way. Usually dignified, serious, and well-dressed, my abba had gotten thoroughly drunk the night before and found it difficult to get up that morning. I was confused when someone had to poke his nose with an acupuncture needle to awaken him. This had never happened before. When he finally arose, Abba collected me in his arms, then took me to the car. It was just the two of us, as if we were running a distant errand together.

"Myung Soo, just wait right here." His voice sounded thick.

I was not alarmed. I had spent most of my six years inside the family home due to the crippling nature of the polio. It had affected the muscles of my legs and my lower back severely; I had never known what it was like to walk and run like my siblings. My mother and father had subjected me to various traditional Eastern medical treatments, but no matter what we tried, my legs remained immobile.

I was still small enough to be carried wherever I couldn't crawl, making use of my arms while dragging my legs. Despite the fact that there were other family problems and much turmoil, my parents had been good to me. So if my abba took me somewhere and told me to wait, he would be back.

The car ride from our home in Seoul had been long. He had brought me out into the countryside, beyond the reach of the city buses, and now we were in front of an unfamiliar low building surrounded by brown dirt. I could hear children's voices somewhere out of sight.

I looked up one more time, but Abba's face was silhouetted against the bright sky, obscuring his expression. He pointed to the steps leading up to the building. "There," Abba ordered. "Crawl over there and cry." He then turned around, and he was gone.

I hoisted my upper body on my arms, not bothering to brush off the dust that clung to them. At least this dirt was not gravelly; dragging myself would be easier. My father had told me what to do. The sun was getting hotter.

After a short time, seeing no one and feeling both hungry and thirsty, I remembered to cry. That's what my abba had said. Then "they" would come. . .

I did not realize until many days later that I had been abandoned. That low building was an orphanage, and it would be my home for the next four years. But I was not an orphan!

1

ABANDONED

Fear not: for I am with thee: I will bring thy seed from the east, and gather thee from the west; I will say to the north, Give up; and to the south, Keep not back: bring my sons from far, and my daughters from the ends of the earth; even every one that is called by my name: for I have created him for my glory, I have formed him; yea, I have made him.

—Isaiah 43:5–7 (KJV)

Every day for several weeks, after eating my breakfast of cornmeal mush, I would crawl through the dirt back to the spot where Abba had left me. What else could I do? I would sit there expectantly and patiently, my scrawny legs coated with powdery dust. The people inside the building were nice to me, and there were many children there, but nobody explained anything to me. *Abba would come back, wouldn't he? Had something bad happened to him?*

Each day, one of the caretakers would eventually come out and take me back inside. After another meal, usually *jook* (rice porridge), they would settle me on my mat and blanket on the floor beside the other little boys, most of whom seemed to have something wrong with their bodies.

I told them my name, Cho Myung Soo, but I did not know anything more to tell them. I did not realize at the time that many Korean parents had been forced to abandon their children to orphanages because of the aftereffects of the Korean War and three years of famine. They simply could not take care of them for one reason or another. The people in charge of the orphanage did their best to meet the needs of all the children.

I had ended up in the Holt orphanage in Ilsan, northwest of the vast city of Seoul, and I would never see my father again.

MY LITTLE SISTER APPEARS

One afternoon, after about a week, someone appeared in the doorway of the general-purpose room, holding the hand of a little girl—my younger sister, Myung Hee! Much later, I found out that my father had sent her along after me so I would not be alone in my abandonment. A relative by marriage of his sister (who apparently had been the one to persuade him to abandon me) had brought Myung Hee and had signed her into the Holt Children's Services center.

"Myung Hee!" I exclaimed.

"So is this your sister?" they asked.

"Yes! Yes! Cho Myung Hee!" (Cho was our family surname.) I felt a slight panic.

Four-year-old Myung Hee was smart enough to try to elude an unwanted fate. She did *not* want to go to the orphanage; she wanted to go home. "No, no! I am *not* his sister!" she insisted. It didn't work. I convinced them that I was indeed her brother, and from then on, Myung

Hee was there. She stayed on the girls' side of the three-room building, but we would see each other every day at meals and playtime.

Once Myung Hee came, I think I finally realized, "Well, this is it—just you and me." But we were too young and uninformed to understand why. We didn't know what was going on. *Where was our family? What must we have done wrong to be punished like this?* Even if someone had explained that our father abandoned us in hopes that our lives might be better, we wouldn't have believed it.

I had never been in trouble before. If anything, I was the much-desired son after my parents' first two children turned out to be daughters. The fact that I had gotten polio had compromised that status, but not seriously. I had been the only boy in the family for about four years, until my baby brother was born shortly after Myung Hee. Three girls and two boys, a mother, and a father. We lived as a family for only a short time. Then we were separated and would never live together again.

Now Myung Hee took it upon herself to look after my welfare, even as I did the same for her. Since I did not have crutches or braces, she would often take hold of my legs and walk me like a wheelbarrow, for fun and faster mobility. She was strong for such a little girl. Of course, with my withered, useless legs, I was lighter than the average boy. Sometimes, she would even carry me piggyback.

Since she was so young when she arrived, my sister doesn't remember as much about the orphanage as I do. She does have one distinct memory of a time when the children were making paper chains for Christmas, and one of the kids crunched hers up. I gave her my best brotherly advice: "Go crunch up his paper chain in return!" Which she did. Even if any of the other kids had siblings in the orphanage (and I don't remember any who did), none of them could have given as much attention to each other as we did.

The able-bodied boys and girls had a different place to sleep, separate from us handicapped kids. We had three main rooms. One side was for the boys, and the other side for the girls, with a common room in the middle. They let my sister stay on the girls' side of my building, even though she was not disabled. I could crawl everywhere. It wasn't a huge place.

At night, after we had been settled on our sleeping mats, I would wait for the other fifteen or twenty boys to fall asleep, then quietly cry to myself. No matter how much time had passed, I couldn't help but think I had done something wrong to cause my father to abandon me.

LIFE IN THE ORPHANAGE

The orphanage was full, but there was always room to accept more children. I don't recall hearing about anyone being turned away due to a lack of space. Sleeping on the floor was not an unusual thing for us, since that's where most people slept in their homes, too. The floors in Korean houses were kept warm in cold weather. Back in the 1950s, almost everyone heated their houses with *yeontan,* big blocks of compressed charcoal with holes bored through them. The hot fire of the burning yeontan was used for cooking as well, with ducts under the floor carrying the heat throughout the house. One yeontan would burn and provide steady heat for about twelve hours, when another one would be placed on top to take over.

Once, the yeontan caused a horrific accident involving one of the severely handicapped girls, whose torso was very rigid and hard to move. She was lying on the floor near where two workers were trying to remove the old yeontan by means of metal rods inserted into the holes. The chunks of fuel would get crumbly after they had burned for a while. In this case, the searing-hot charcoal broke apart and fell on the helpless body of the disabled girl. She was screaming with pain, badly burned, and unable to move and get it off of her.

Apart from accidents like that, though, we were comfortable and safe. We slept side-by-side on the floor, as close as sardines in a tin. Outside, it may have been cold, but inside, we were warm. We had no privacy nor any place for personal possessions. Not that we owned anything anyway, except the clothes on our backs. We would bathe outdoors, and we would eat in the common area. The water outside was cold. The orphanage workers would heat it in the wintertime, but never during the summer. We would run the water from the pump into a bucket, then take soap and wash ourselves.

Most of the time, the orphanage kept the handicapped kids separate from the other children. All of us were of school age; I do not remember any babies there.

We were fed regularly, but we were always hungry. During this time, many children living in Korea didn't have much to eat. In hindsight, I was very blessed to be in the orphanage, where I was fed regularly. I later learned that my aunt had a friend who worked in the orphanage, and she made sure we were well taken care of.

Most days, the food was the same and pretty boring: the same cornmeal mush and rice porridge. Boys will be boys and hungry boys go to drastic lengths to make their stomachs stop growling. One day, we stole some old cookies we found in the kitchen. They were crawling with maggots, but that did not stop us. We just picked out the maggots and ate the cookies. Another time, we swiped a stick of butter and shared it.

In search of entertainment as well as food, we would catch snakes, start a little fire, and cook them to eat. Sometimes we got potatoes from a nearby field and ate those, too. For extra protein, we'd roast dragonflies and grasshoppers. Don't ask me how we made the cooking fires or how we got away with that. Sometimes, we would catch and kill rats, bashing their heads with rocks. We didn't eat those though. Children who have been abandoned and are famished have the instinct to eat just about anything, in an attempt to fill the emptiness in their hearts as well as their stomachs.

The orphanage was surrounded by wetlands. There was a small pond that would freeze in the winter and we would play on the ice. With a pole, I could push myself around on whatever kind of sled I could find—it was fun to move around so freely.

We would go swimming in that same pond on hot summer days. I remember one time, some kids were playing in the water, but I couldn't join in because I didn't know how to swim. A bigger kid said, "Just hold onto my neck and I'll walk around the pond, okay?" I was holding onto him when he suddenly slipped. Amidst the chaos, I managed to grab onto what felt like a ladder. Thankfully, I didn't drown that day. After that, I made sure I learned how to swim at the first opportunity.

Frogs were all over the place in that wet environment. Once, we had a bunch of them in a jar. I remember I had gotten into trouble for something, and the house mother banned me from attending movie night, which took place at a church on the orphanage property. Needless to say, I didn't like that, so I threw a fit and argued with her.

When that didn't work, I tried to bribe her. "If I give you some gum, can I go?"

Her answer was firm. "No. You are being punished." So as soon as she left the room, I let all the frogs out of the jar.

Looking back, I don't think we always had an adult watching us. We must have been on our own a lot of the time if we were able to get into so much mischief!

At first, none of the handicapped children were permitted to attend school, but after I received some donated crutches, I was allowed to begin my education since I could now walk to class. This was a welcome development, but only up to a point. The kids at school picked on me mercilessly. All I could do was throw my crutches at them, which only made them laugh harder. Then I would return to the orphanage and take out my frustration and anger on my disabled roommates. The nondisabled orphans who attended school with me would go off to their separate living quarters at the end of the day. Nobody stood up for me. I simply had to look after myself.

(There were many disabled orphans who could never live independently, so the Ilsan orphanage eventually expanded and became a rehabilitation and residential center for disabled adults. It still exists today, operating under the auspices of the Holt Children's Services of Korea.)

We had very little in the way of medical care. I do remember one major surgery, an operation on my hip and to fuse my right ankle, at the U.S. military hospital in Korea. This was an entirely new experience for me. The only attempts at medical care I had received before coming to the orphanage had been quite traumatic, consisting of burning my skin with little sticks, like herbal cigarettes—traditional Chinese and Korean moxibustion—in failed attempts to stimulate the damaged nerves in my legs and back. I bear the scars to this day.

My sister and I were not the only ones in the orphanage who were not true orphans. Besides the handicapped children of Korean parents who simply could not provide for them, there were kids whose fathers were American G.I.s. When the U.S. troops departed, they had left behind many single mothers raising half-Korean children. These biracial Amerasian "G.I. babies" looked different, and they were very much discriminated against. Whether their fathers had been fair-skinned

Caucasians or African-Americans, these kids were called "other sheep." Nobody wanted them. Their mothers were stigmatized, too, because Korean society does not show much tolerance for single mothers. That's why so many of these kids ended up in our orphanage.

The adult workers at the orphanage would come and go. We children didn't pay much attention to whether they lived on the premises or elsewhere. In Korean, they were called *bo-mos,* or "caring mothers," with *bo* meaning "caring" and *mo* meaning "mother." Some of them were older women while others were very young, like nannies. We could tell that they were a little more educated than the cooks. The bo-mos knew how to take care of little children, and the cooks did not. The cooks stayed in the kitchen area.

UNADOPTABLE...IN MORE WAYS THAN ONE

I knew I was in an orphanage, I understood the name "Holt," and I was aware that some of the workers came from the United States, but no one ever told me about the possibility of being adopted into a family—in either Korea or America. In all likelihood, that is because my sister and I had too many counts against us where adoption was concerned.

First of all, Korean families were not usually looking for children to adopt, especially not from orphanages, where it was assumed children were getting socialized poorly. Kids who came from orphanages were distrusted, thought to be dishonest and shrewd like street kids. In any case, Koreans would rarely adopt in order to expand their nuclear families, preferring to incorporate an orphan into their households in the role of a conscripted servant.

Beyond that reality for me and my sister was the further complication of being older children. Myung Hee and I were no longer cute little babies. And we were siblings—who would ever want both of us? Then there was the biggest drawback of all—my polio. If my own father and mother could not figure out how to take care of me, how could strangers do it? And international adoption? Why would anyone from America even take a second look at us? We were not very "adoptable" at all.

Still, we had landed in a good place, all things considered. We weren't on the streets, and we were still alive and growing well. I now know that God Himself had His hand firmly on our lives.

THE HOLT ORPHANAGES

The orphanage was Christian. I can't say the same for our home, but the Christian features of orphanage life did not seem foreign to me. I remember seeing crosses on the walls there. I didn't really know who Jesus was, but I was motivated to memorize all sixty-six books of the Bible so I could earn a Bible of my own. This was in the context of some kind of Sunday-school-like time they had in the orphanage. We would sing Christian songs, hymns, and Christmas carols.

The story of the orphanage is interesting and inspiring, although I didn't know the details until later.[1] Harry Holt, the founder of the Ilsan orphanage, was the father of six children with his wife, Bertha, who was a nurse. After the Depression, they had moved from an Iowa farm to Oregon, where Harry worked hard and became a successful sawmill owner. After a heart attack in 1950 gave him a brush with death, he went back to farming, this time in Oregon. He provided well for his family, and they were quite content together.

In 1954, Bob Pierce, the founder of the child-sponsoring organization, World Vision, came to the local church to show a couple of films. His goal was to recruit more sponsors—people who would pledge ten dollars a month to sponsor a needy child in a country such as Korea. At first, Harry didn't want to go to the event, but his kids—including his

1. See: Bertha Holt, David Wisner, *The Seed from the East* (Oxford, England: The Oxford Press, 1956). The book includes conversations with members of the Holt family.

daughter Molly, who ended up dedicating her life to helping Korean orphans—persuaded him to attend.

When Harry saw the film called *The Other Sheep*, he couldn't believe what was going on in Korea after the Korean War. After seeing the pictures of the war orphans, he was so moved that he sponsored as many children as he could through World Vision.

But sponsoring children was not enough. The very next year, Harry and Bertha Holt decided to adopt eight Korean orphans—all at once—modifying their large home to accommodate them. International adoption was virtually unheard of at the time. After initiating the process of obtaining the required refugee-immigrant visas by special permission from Washington, D.C., Harry went in person to Korea in 1955 to locate adoptable children and bring them back. On his way, sick and discouraged and seeking confirmation that this was indeed the will of God, he opened the King James Bible to Isaiah 43:5–7, which reads:

> *Fear not: for I am with thee: I will bring thy seed from the east, and gather thee from the west; I will say to the north, Give up; and to the south, Keep not back: bring my sons from far, and my daughters from the ends of the earth; even every one that is called by my name: for I have created him for my glory, I have formed him; yea, I have made him.*

After many delays and much effort, he came home with eight boys and girls, who were welcomed with open arms into the Holt family. The older children were delighted with their new brothers and sisters, and they all pitched in to help their parents take care of them.

Harry's extraordinary accomplishment made the news in a big way, and queries started to come in from couples everywhere, wanting to know how they, too, could adopt Korean orphans. Thus, Harry decided to return to Korea to see what he could do to provide for the neglected children there. His health was not the best, and he did not like to be separated from his wife and family so much, but urged on by the flood of queries from prospective adoptive parents, in 1956 (the year I was born), he returned to the needy country that had captured his heart. Only a few months after bringing home his eight new children, he started to organize an adoption program. Now, to make it a reality, he needed to figure out how to house the potential adoptees in Korea.

Meanwhile, back home in Oregon, Bertha and her older daughters started handling the American end of the adoption process, hiring several people to help. The Orphan Foundation Fund was incorporated in late 1956; the name was later changed to the Holt Adoption Program. Within a few years, most of the older Holt children got married or moved to pursue adult careers, but after being apart from Harry more than she was with him, Bertha eventually brought the rest of their large brood to Korea to join him. Their temporary quarters were grossly insufficient, so Harry—the farmer that he was—purchased a tractor and began to work on what would become the orphanage in Ilsan—the one to which I was taken in 1962. This site was chosen because it was undeveloped, unlike property closer to the city of Seoul. The whole time I was living there, the property was being developed further, and improvements have continued to be made right up to the present time.

Harry Holt's health finally broke under the strain. He literally worked himself to death, pressing on with both the building and the adoptions all the more because he seemed to realize that his time was short. He died in 1964 in Ilsan, having sent Bertha and their "second family" back to Oregon. Thanks to his extraordinary efforts (and to at least one unexpectedly mild winter), the entire Ilsan orphanage—which consisted at that time of forty buildings and was expected to take ten years to finish—had been completed in only twenty-eight months.

After Harry died, Bertha, nicknamed "Grandma (*Halmoni*) Holt," shouldered the burden of steering the leadership of the orphanage and the adoption program, which had grown so much that it involved many others. Several of her adult children helped, too, including Molly, who stayed more than fifty years and is still serving there today. Today, Holt International Children's Services operates adoption programs in seven countries in addition to Korea and works with adoptive families in all fifty of the United States. I remain eternally grateful for everything the Holts did for me and so many other children.

Although Harry was the first hero of the story, Bertha became the much-loved matriarch of the every-growing Holt outreach. When she died in 2000 at the age of ninety-six, her funeral in Korea was attended by a thousand people. It was like a state occasion, with the president's wife in attendance and a special motorcade from the Seoul airport to escort her casket when it arrived from America. She is buried beside Harry on top of a hill overlooking the Ilsan complex.

By the time of Bertha's funeral, I had been living in the United States for thirty-four years. My attendance at that funeral marked a crucial decision-point in my life.

ABANDON HOPE, ALL YE WHO ENTER HERE

The whole time I was in the orphanage, from the age of six until the age of ten, I never saw any of the other disabled kids get adopted. I wasn't aware of very many adoptions of healthy children either. My sister and I simply adjusted to our new life with no particular expectations.

It was as if the motto posted over the gateway to Dante's hell, from his epic poem *The Divine Comedy*, had been posted over the door to the orphanage: "Abandon hope, all ye who enter here." Well, it wasn't quite as bad as that because they did do their best to take care of us. But the word "hope" was not really a part of my working vocabulary. I merely lived from one day to the next like any child, although without any assurance of the future. The workers were nice, but nobody explained anything to us because they didn't know what to say. *Whose children were we? Where were our families? Where would we go when we grew up?* We had no answers to these questions.

If only I'd been given a sixty-cent dose of polio vaccine, none of this would have happened.

2

LIFE SENTENCE

When Jesus heard it he said,
"This illness does not lead to death. It is for the glory of God,
so that the Son of God may be glorified through it."
—John 11:4 (ESV)

Imagine what it would be like to wake up some morning and discover that you cannot walk. That's what happened to Franklin Delano Roosevelt in 1921. "It's polio," his doctors said. He was thirty-nine years old, a healthy, wealthy husband and father. And for the rest of his life, he was completely dependent upon other people for assistance.

Most often, polio strikes growing children, but it also can afflict adults. I was infected by the virus as a baby, yet I cannot say which is worse: to begin your life under the permanent aftereffects of infantile paralysis (an older name for polio) or to be cut down in the prime of life. Either way, polio is a devastating life sentence.

In the case of FDR, who had already launched his career as a public servant and had plenty of money with which to pay for therapies and assistance, the miracle is that he carried on for as long and as well as he did. He went on to win the presidency of the United States a record four times in a row, carrying the nation through the end of the Depression and most of World War II. He already had a wife and children; one of his sons served as his personal assistant for many years.

But he learned early, as I did, that a disability such as polio changes the way people treat you. It's inevitable. Your wheelchair, your crutches, your posture, your overall inability to navigate the everyday world alongside others—all of them label you as "handicapped," "disabled," or whatever term is in current use.

In FDR's case, he took great pains to compensate, lest the American people decide that his fitness for office was as enfeebled as his legs were. Have you ever noticed how very few photographs show Roosevelt in a wheelchair? He always managed to stand up at podiums to make speeches and he is pictured greeting crowds while seated in a convertible. The public knew he had trouble walking, but he would have been sidelined if people had known the full extent of his incapacity.

I have learned the same thing. Like anyone who requires assistance to achieve mobility, I have firsthand experience of being ignored by strangers, as if my ability to communicate must be compromised as much as my ability to walk. My wheelchair, as much as I need it at times, creates a particular set of problems beyond navigating ramps and opening doors. When I use a wheelchair to shop in a big store, with my wife Sook Hee pushing it, store employees are much less likely to talk directly to me. I may ask the question, but the retail personnel prefer to answer my wife, who is standing. They look right over my head and reply to her as if she had made the request! *How does that work?* I wonder. "Hey, I asked the question and I'm down here!" It's as if I am an inanimate object, a part of the chair I'm sitting in. However, if I am standing up beside her, this doesn't happen. Even the presence of my crutches does not have the same effect as that wheelchair does. When

I'm sitting down, I guess they think I'm a total invalid. That's just one small example of how different it is to function as a disabled person in an "abled" world.

When I travel, I always wear a sport coat because when I require wheelchair assistance in an airport, I am treated better. Somehow, that one article of clothing makes me seem more intelligent or important, more deserving of respect.

People just don't know how to relate to people with disabilities. The sight of my paralyzed legs seems to paralyze *them*. That's why I always try to be friendly. If little kids are staring, I'll explain. "Hey, you know why I have crutches? When I was in kindergarten, I didn't get my kindergarten shots. So when you go to kindergarten, be sure to get your shots, even though they hurt a little bit, and you won't get sick like me and have to use crutches."

I try to make people feel comfortable around me by going ahead to do whatever I need to do, unselfconsciously, even if others are bothered somewhat. A lot of times when I go swimming and people see my stunted legs, they say, "Hey, I admire you. You're just doing what you can." It starts some good conversations about how God gives each of us only one body, and we need to take care of it as well as we can.

FINDING THE RIGHT WORDS

I admire the people who lobby and work for disabled rights, although that is not really the focus of my energy. But I certainly appreciate the many benefits of living in the United States of America, especially when I return from a trip overseas. It's hard enough to manage wherever I am and I notice my limitations much more now that I'm older. When you consider the challenges for able-bodied people doing even the simplest things in an underdeveloped country, you can see how the advantages of living in the handicap-accessible United States stack up so favorably. Even in well-to-do Western nations, I find too many stairs and not enough elevators.

It's often hard for people to find the appropriate terminology to talk about disabilities, whether or not they are trying to be politically correct. We have set aside terms such as "crippled" and "retarded" in favor of words and phrases that recognize the dignity of the individual. At the same time, sometimes we go overboard ("differently-abled"), applying words such as "brave" indiscriminately, or referring to non-disabled people as "normal" or "healthy"—which of course implies that those of us with disabilities are *ab*normal and *un*healthy, across the board.

Not long ago, I was invited to a banquet sponsored by an organization that is working to eradicate polio. My table place card read, "Steve Stirling, polio victim." Please, no! I never was a victim and I am not a victim today. I may be a polio survivor, but I prefer to be simply a man named Steve Stirling.

I don't mind the word handicapped and I will use it in this book. "Disabled" is fine. "On crutches" is even better. Technically, polio made me a paraplegic. Polio has defined my life in many ways, but I would rather talk about it in terms of how God allowed it to happen so that He could be glorified. That is my ultimate aim.

WHAT IS POLIO?

People don't think about polio as often as they used to now that the disease has been largely conquered globally with vaccines, and those of us who are living with the aftereffects make up a much smaller proportion of the population.[2]

2. The United States was declared polio-free in 1979. However, a similar disease has cropped up in the news. It is known as Acute Flaccid Myelitis (AFM), a "polio-like illness" that seems to affect children only. Despite having infected several hundred children in the United States, it remains a rare nervous system disease and its cause, prevention, and treatment are still being evaluated and developed. See "Polio-Like Illness Strikes Kids, Frustrates Doctors" Oct. 18, 2019, WebMD (https://www.webmd.com/children/news/20181019/polio-like-illness-strikes-kids-frustrates-doctors).

"Polio" is short for poliomyelitis, a sometimes-deadly disease caused by the poliovirus, which spreads in much the same way as other viruses, from one person to another. Often, infected people do not know they have contracted the disease because their symptoms are relatively mild, like a case of the flu, and they go away without treatment—or they may have no symptoms at all. But when the virus invades the cells of a person's spinal cord and brain, it can cause paralysis. Obviously, this is what happened to me.

The word *poliomyelitis* means "inflammation of gray marrow," from the Greek words *polios* (gray) and *myelos* (marrow), along with the suffix *-itis,* which indicates inflammation. The virus destroys nerve cells, the "gray marrow," in a person's spinal cord, which disrupts the transmission of signals from the brain to the muscles. The affected muscles will manifest the damage in a range of ways, from slight weakness of one arm or leg to total paralysis of arms, legs, diaphragm, and chest muscles. Even though it affects brain impulses, it rarely causes sensory loss.

Usually, the paralysis involves the arms or legs, as in my case. In about 10 percent of people paralyzed by polio, the ability to breathe is affected and these patients are the most likely to die. Back in the 1950s, some of them had to resort to "iron lungs" because the paralyzed muscles in their chests prevented them from breathing on their own.

Only a few iron lungs still exist; the only one I have ever seen is in the museum at the federal Centers for Disease Control and Prevention (CDC) in Atlanta, Georgia.[3] Only when the disease actually results in some kind of paralysis is it defined as "polio."

Polio has always been around wherever human populations gather. There is even an Egyptian carved stone slab that depicts a man and one

3. The Centers for Disease Control and Prevention (CDC) is a branch of the U.S. Department of Health and Human Services. "Iron lung" is the common name of the Emerson respirator, which was invented in the 1920s. It was phased out in 1970, although a small handful of elderly patients still use it today.

of his legs looks a lot like mine. But polio became a fearful scourge when people began to flock to big cities, where they often lived in crowded, unsanitary conditions. Around 1900, polio epidemics started to occur in the warm summer months all over the world. One of the worst outbreaks happened around the time I was born, in the 1940s through the 1950s. In those years, notably in 1949, it's estimated that more than 500,000 people a year were paralyzed or killed worldwide. The United States was hard hit.

FOR LACK OF A SIMPLE VACCINATION

After I was an adult and got in touch with some members of my birth family, I found out from my biological mother how I had contracted the disease. Apparently, my father had attended a funeral for the son of one of his friends. Unbeknownst to my dad, the boy had died of polio. At the funeral, my father must have picked up the virus from his friend, or some other symptom-free family member, and then brought it home to me, his own baby son. I can hardly imagine the terrible load of guilt he must have carried as he tried to care for me as well as he could.

This was in 1957, the first year the polio vaccine became widely available in the United States and other western countries. Developed by researcher Jonas Salk, the inactivated poliovirus was injected into the arm or leg. However, it was not available in war-torn Korea. (I remember other vaccinations in Korea at that time. Because it was a poverty-stricken, developing country, the nurses would use the same needle over and over, just wiping it off between injections until it got so dull, they couldn't use it anymore.)

Today, the polio vaccine is a routine part of children's preventive health care and it has been administered in many cases in the oral form, which was originated by Albert Sabin in 1961. Because the oral polio vaccine does not involve an injection, it does not require medical personnel, so even nonmedical volunteers can be trained to dispense it. The vaccine has become very inexpensive: only fourteen cents per dose in most cases. Babies can receive their first dose as young as six to eight weeks old.

According to the World Health Organization (WHO), we have eradicated polio globally as much as 99 percent. There are three strains of the wild poliovirus and all of them will die out when they can no longer find an unvaccinated person to infect. (The disease infects humans only, not animals.) The good news is that two strains of polio have been effectively wiped out. Now, to finish the task, national governments have banded together with five partners who martial millions of volunteers across the globe.

Polio was vanquished in the Western Hemisphere in 1994, thanks to aggressive vaccination campaigns and comprehensive compliance of children and their parents. Still, until polio is eradicated from the face of the earth, anybody who has not been vaccinated is susceptible, especially with all of today's air travel.

Suppose you visit India and bring the virus home to a young child who hasn't yet had the vaccine. Suddenly, polio has been reintroduced to the United States, and others who have not received the vaccine are vulnerable. We have to be vigilant in our efforts to wipe it out.

POLIO IN THE ORPHANAGE

In the orphanage, I remember two or three other boys who were in a situation similar to mine, with the lower part of their bodies affected. Part of the reason I remember is that when my sister and I were playing and did the "wheelbarrow walk," they got someone to grab their legs to walk that way, too. I know we also had kids with cerebral palsy and mental disabilities. None of us were confined to bed—well, we slept on the floor anyway. My childhood memories don't include every detail, but

I have the impression that some of those kids had been there well before I got there in 1962, possibly since the founding of the orphanage around the time I was born.

When we kids with polio arrived, we had nothing to help us get around, like crutches. We crawled, pulling our legs behind us, or scooted forward. I think it must have taken a couple of years before I got crutches, so I might have been about seven or eight years old by then. Obtaining crutches almost certainly depended on the amount of extra support money that came in. I think the other kids got crutches about the same time I did. Then after a while, we all got leg braces, too. Even though those braces helped us stand with our crutches, we hated those things because they were so uncomfortable. One of the workers, whose name was Sally Mack, used to scold me for not wearing my braces: "Put your braces on, Myung Soo!"

With both crutches and braces, I learned to walk long distances without getting tired. That degree of mobility has served me well, even as walking with crutches has worn out my shoulder joints over the years.

I got used to wearing braces, but I still have a love/hate relationship with them, and I take them off as soon as I come home from work; I don't need them to get around the house. Like FDR, whose braces were much heavier and more painfully cumbersome than mine, I really enjoy swimming because then I can take the braces off and move freely, completely without assistance.

The parts of my body that have been paralyzed by polio have needed all the help they can get, and surgery has been one of the options. The people at the orphanage arranged for me to have my first two surgeries while I was still under their care. After that, I had at least eight more surgeries while I was still a child. Most of them took place in Alaska after I was adopted by a family there. The most extensive one—to insert "Harrington rods" in my back—kept me in a Shriner's hospital in Oregon for months.

Each surgical procedure was designed to reinforce the parts of my body that had been badly weakened by the polio I contracted as an infant. Even as a little boy, I knew the operations would be worth the pain they entailed.

JUST A THROWAWAY KID

Because I was only one year old when I got polio, I do not remember life before it. I was born into an ordinary Korean family that was neither poor nor wealthy, and no amount of money would have made it possible for my parents to alleviate the many complications that my affliction presented. The same situation has been played out across the world. The circumstances and prospects for children with disabilities in developing countries are truly horrific. They have a hard life. They are ostracized as untouchables.

After I was abandoned, I felt the reality of my situation for the first time. Nobody had to teach me to keep my fears and tears to myself. I was on my own. When I wept silently on my sleeping mat in the dark, I would also cry out to God. Night after night, I would usually fall asleep talking to Him. I didn't really know much about Him, but I didn't have anyone else to talk to. I knew He was listening then and I know it even better now, because He truly answered my heartfelt prayers.

Although I did not understand until much later, the cries of my heart were echoing the eternal words of the ancient psalms:

> *The unfortunate commits himself to You; You have been the helper of the orphan.* (Psalm 10:14 NASB)

> *You have seen me tossing and turning through the night. You have collected all my tears and preserved them in your bottle! You have recorded every one in your book.... I am trusting God—oh, praise his promises! I am not afraid of anything mere man can do to me!... Thank you for your help. For you have saved me from death and my feet from slipping, so that I can walk before the Lord in the land of the living.* (Psalm 56:8, 10–13, 12–13 TLB)

Today, I know how securely I was held in God's strong hands, even in the darkest times. He heard my every cry and He made sure that I would be wonderfully saved from my lonely plight.

3

LOOKING UP

God decided in advance to adopt us into his own family by bringing us to himself through Jesus Christ. This is what he wanted to do, and it gave him great pleasure.
—Ephesians 1:5 (NLT)

The United States was still reeling from the assassination of John F. Kennedy, the Vietnam War was escalating, and South Korean President Park Chung-hee was being harassed by student demonstrators. Living day-to-day in the Ilsan orphanage, my sister and I were unaware of any of this. It was 1964 and Lyndon Johnson was the president of the United States. Mid-year, he signed the Civil Rights Act, officially abolishing racial segregation. Shortly afterward, Martin Luther King Jr. received the Nobel Peace Prize. The Mariner 4 space probe was on its way to the planet Mars, and the Beatles were singing "I Want to Hold Your Hand." But Myung Hee and I knew nothing of the outside world. We also had no clue that our lives were about to change again in a big way.

Except for my crutches, I acted like a typical eight-year-old Korean boy, going to school and getting into mischief. My sister and I continued to look out for each other's welfare in the crowded orphanage. She was six and very spunky. All things considered, we were doing all right.

But one great need loomed like a big black cloud over our lives: we wanted more than anything to be part of a real family again. Myung Hee could barely remember our family home, but I could. The pain of our abrupt and inexplicable removal from all things near and dear had barely diminished for me in the two years we had lived at the Holt orphanage. Even a single year can seem very long to a child. *My father loved me, so why did he send me away? What had happened to him? To our mother? To our big sisters and little brother?*

Of course, all of the children in the orphanage had the same yearning for a family. Once in a while, a lucky one would be adopted, thanks to the efforts of the Holts, who were always making new connections with adoptive parents in the United States. But my sister and I did not dare to dream of being so fortunate, fenced in as we were by the many counts against us. We knew our chances for adoption were very low—really zero—and our prospects would not improve as we got older.

A GROUNDBREAKING DECISION

Harry and Bertha Holt had adopted eight Korean War orphans in 1955, which changed everything. They had to get special permission from the federal government to do so, with their children being considered war refugees. An amendment to the Refugee Relief Act of 1953 enabled them to continue to bring children to the United States for adoption, but it was not without controversy as they bypassed the established standards of U.S. child welfare regulations in favor of extricating as many children as possible from poverty and neglect. The Holts' eight adopted children were all G.I. babies, as were many of the others who they brought to the United States. In fact, so many U.S. soldiers had abandoned (or had never known about) their offspring in Korea that the children's plight captured the attention of many prospective parents.

The Holts' groundbreaking work is now an established part of the history of international adoption in the United States, as illustrated by this excerpt from a Brandeis University report:

> The wide spread of international adoption began in 1955, when Henry and Bertha Holt, an evangelical couple from rural Oregon, secured a special act of Congress enabling them to adopt Korean "war orphans." These children of Korean women and American G.I.s had been stigmatized or abandoned because of their visible ethnic differences and the presumption of infidelity or illegitimacy. The Holts turned their personal experience into a mission, founding the first organization dedicated to large-scale international adoption, Holt International Children's Services, which still exists today.[4]

When Harry Holt died in 1964, adoptions from Korea slowed temporarily. But his wife and family carried on, and others shared the burdens involved in the complex adoption process and lobbied Congress for new and more generous regulations.

In 1966, when Bertha Holt was named Mother of the Year by the American Mothers Committee of the Golden Rule Foundation, adoptions picked up again due to the publicity. The following glowing summary of her accomplishments regarding international adoption was published in her honor:

> Bertha Holt was born in a happy, Christian home in Des Moines, Iowa in 1904 and graduated from the University of

4. From "Capsule History of International Adoption," © 2008-2014 Schuster Institute for Investigative Journalism, Brandeis University, Waltham, MA, 02454 (https://www.brandeis.edu/investigate/adoption/history.html).

Iowa with a Bachelor's degree in nursing. After working for a year and a half in the nursing profession, she married Harry Holt, a South Dakota farmer. Bertha became active in 4-H work and in Public Health. She and Harry had four children in South Dakota, and two more after they moved to Oregon, where Harry entered the lumber industry. Both were dedicated to the Christian faith and when their six children ranged in age from nine to twenty years, they learned of the plight of thousands of Korean orphans, most of who were illegitimate children of G.I.s from the war.

Harry flew over to Korea to see the situation for himself and returned with eight Korean children for them to adopt. They encountered considerable legal challenges, but the vision of little children dying in gutters, starving and unloved, haunted this compassionate couple. So, with prayers and unbelievable courage, they established an adoption agency at home and went in search of an orphanage for the 400 children who, for health reasons, could not be accepted into the United States. With their incredible sacrifice and perseverance, by 1966 over 3,000 Korean orphans had been placed in American homes.[5]

Even though we were not G.I. babies, my sister and I became two of those fortunate Korean orphans.

ENTER JIM AND LYN STIRLING

Jim and Lyn Stirling had always wanted a big family—at least four children—because Jim had grown up as an only child and Lyn had only one brother. When they did not seem to be able to conceive a baby, they adopted two American children, five-year-old Dale and three-day-old

5. From "1966 Mother of the Year" (published May 5, 1966), archived on the American Mothers, Inc., website at https://www.americanmothers.org/1966-national-mother-of-the-year.

infant Patty, and made their home in Pasadena, California. Then, inspired by a neighbor who had adopted a couple of Korean children, they decided to do the same. They wanted their children to grow up with several siblings.

Through Holt Children's Services, they were matched with a boy and a girl who lived in our orphanage in Ilsan. That's what brought them there in 1964. They came in person to pick up their two new Korean children, renamed Bob and Teresa, who were about five and three years old.

Before they came, they had been advised to bring a bag of candy to distribute to all of the other orphans who would be left behind. Standing beside an orphanage worker, they passed out candy to the thronging kids, most of whom immediately popped it into their mouths, some even holding out their hands for more.

But my sister, Myung Hee, darted up to the tall American couple with a smile, closed her fist around her candy, and then ran off so quickly that the Stirlings took notice of it.

"Why did she just run off like that? Is she afraid of us?"

"Not that one," said the orphanage employee. "Myung Hee has a disabled brother and she is taking him candy first. She always shares everything with him."

Spontaneously, both Stirlings said, "We must go in and meet them. May we?" After they finished handing out the rest of the candy, the employee led them to the area where the disabled children were kept.

Lyn would later say, "Myung Hee and Myung Soo came over to us immediately and hugged us and stayed with us. Jim and I just looked at each other and raised our eyebrows. And that was it."

To our astonishment, before they left with Bob and Teresa, the Stirlings took my sister and me aside and told us that they wanted to be our parents! They made it clear that the process might take a long time, but they promised to do everything possible to bring us home with them to America.

This was not going to be easy. Under federal law at that time, an American couple was only allowed to adopt two international children. Before they could adopt two more, the Stirlings were going to have to get the law changed. Undaunted, they brought Bob and Teresa back home with them to California and began to write letters to lobby the legislators who could make it happen.

They really meant it. In their letters to us, they promised Myung Hee and me that they would come back for us as soon as possible. (Eventually, we were renamed Mary Ellen and Steven Glenn.) It was miracle! We were going to be part of a family again. Somebody *loved* us.

A NEW LIFE GUARANTEE

To help Stirlings' promise to adopt us come true, I decided to already think of them as Mom and Dad and write letters to them. At six, my sister was too young to compose letters, but at eight, I knew how to write well enough in Korean to do so. The orphanage personnel encouraged me, helped me obtain writing materials, and translated and mailed the letters for me. The letter-writing really helped to build up my anticipation about coming to the United States.

My mother kept my letters. Here is an excerpt from one, written in childish Korean characters, with a typewritten translation to English provided by one of the bilingual orphanage staff members:

Saturday March 6, 1965

Dear mother,

How are you mother? I am very fine. My sister is well too. Mother, I am now the third year. We learn English and songs. I feel hard to walk to school. But I am so glad that I could have the treatment for my leg. I read your letter. Mother, I'll have to close for now. Good-bye, mother!

Love, Cho Myung Soon [my name was misspelled]

Our new parents wrote back many times over the long months, and they sent gifts, too. They really wanted us! Hoping against hope, we believed with all our hearts that someday, we would go to America to be with them. We had always heard about America, the land of milk and honey. America was *mee-gook*, the Korean pronunciation of the Chinese characters for "the beautiful country." We did not really know what it would be like there, but that didn't matter to us.

Much later in my life, I came to understand the significance of the word "adoption" to people who have faith in God and Jesus:

> *For those who are led by the Spirit of God are the children of God. The Spirit you received does not make you slaves, so that you live in fear again; rather, the Spirit you received brought about your adoption to sonship. And by him we cry, "Abba, Father."*
>
> (Romans 8:14–15 NIV)

A believer's new life in Christ Jesus should be very different from his or her old life lived under restless personal effort. Like the two of us waiting in the Korean orphanage, believers feel that their future in a completely new place is assured. Even though you and I can barely understand what it is like to live in the kingdom of God here on earth (and still less to live in heaven), we want it with all our hearts and we freely offer ourselves to be adopted by our heavenly Father, for "*God is love*" (1 John 4:8 NIV). Who wouldn't want to find new life with the most loving Father of them all?

MAKING BIG MOVES

Right in the midst of all of the lobbying and letter-writing, Jim Stirling, who was an engineer, got a new oil-industry job with the government…in Anchorage, Alaska. That's a long way from southern California! So they packed their Volkswagen bus with their luggage, their four kids, a black Labrador, a cat, and a canary in a cage, and drove north.

It was a punishing journey. This was before the Alaska Highway (then known as the Alaska-Canada Highway or "Alcan") was completed. After they left behind the paved roads of Washington State and British Columbia, crossing into the Canadian Yukon, much of the road was unimproved, potholed gravel. Many flat tires later, they arrived safely and bought a small house. They had moved north only a short time after the huge earthquake hit Anchorage on Good Friday, March 27, 1964. It was a time of tremendous upheaval for everyone!

From their new home, they renewed their campaign to get permission to adopt us. At last, after two years of letter-writing and advocacy on the part of people of influence, President Lyndon B. Johnson signed into law the bill that would lift the restriction. I have a photocopy of it in my possession today: "H.R. [House of Representatives] 8219, May 17, 1965…. A Bill for the relief of Cho Myung Soon and Cho Myung Hee. *Be it enacted by the Senate and House of Representatives of the United States of America in Congress assembled,* That, in the administration of the Immigration and Nationality Act, Cho Myung Soon and Cho Myung Hee may be classified as eligible orphans within the meaning of section 101(b) (1) (F) of the Act, upon approval of a petition filed in their behalf by Mr. and Mrs. Alexander J. Stirling, citizens of the United States..." Mom and Dad could legally adopt us. We could go home at last!

The last evening before we left Korea, someone took us to a Korean restaurant for a nice meal. That was a new experience. It made me remember eating that kind of food, including meat, fish, and other good things, when I was still with my family. To this day, despite many traumatic memories of my country of origin, I do enjoy Korean food.

We would travel in one of the airplanes that the Holts chartered to ferry children, along with their temporary caretakers, to the States. I later found out that my sister and I were escorted by an Alaskan man who was a friend of my future wife's aunt. Hardly looking back, we said good-bye to the other children and the orphanage workers.

We went to the airport in Seoul and from there, we flew to Tokyo and then all the way across the ocean to Anchorage. Of course, the flight would be our first; we were both scared and excited. In honor of the occasion, our new parents sent us new clothes to wear for the journey. I remember putting on my spiffy Cub Scout uniform for the trip. I was ten years old and Mary Ellen was eight.

Even our unexpected airsickness on the turbulent ocean crossing could not dim our enthusiasm. We hardly uttered a word, glued to the windows with wide eyes. Everything was new. Things were definitely looking up.

4

STERLING STIRLINGS

God sets the lonely in families,
he leads out the prisoners with singing.
—Psalm 68:6 (NIV)

Our plane jolted as it touched down in Anchorage.

Mary Ellen and I pressed our faces against the windows. "Did you see the huge ocean? Look at those mountains!" How big the mountains were! We had never seen snow-covered peaks before. It was the end of summer, yet they still had snow on them. America the beautiful!

Stepping off the plane, we squinted in the bright sunshine. The air smelled so fresh. What a contrast to the pollution we had left behind in Seoul. And there was our family, waving to us. Dale, Bob, Teresa, and little Patty. Mom and Dad got down on their knees and scooped us into their arms. They took us to the parking lot, where the eight of us squeezed into a red and white Volkswagen bus with Dad behind the wheel. On the way home, we stopped at a grocery store. While the rest of us stayed in the car, Mom went in to buy some things. Then we went home.

Home was a small, three-bedroom, one-bathroom house. I was going to share a room with my two brothers. They gave me the lower part of the bunk bed. I felt very welcomed.

The sole bathroom was in constant use. Pity the poor kid who had "held it" until the end of a family outing in the car! (Sometimes, we boys would solve that problem by all going at the same time.) For the six years we all lived together in that house, the week's bathing schedule was regimented: Mondays, Wednesdays, and Fridays were the boys' nights; Tuesdays, Thursdays, and Saturdays were for the girls. I'm not sure where Mom and Dad fit into that picture, but somehow, they did.

It was wonderful just to be in the house and realize: *this is our family now*. We didn't know English yet, so initially, we just made gestures, but we learned pretty fast. Because we were young, it was not very difficult for us.

Actually, as soon as we landed in Alaska, Mary Ellen and I vowed to each other, "We will not speak Korean to each other again." We wanted to forget the past. It was too painful. Even while we were still learning English, we refused to resort to Korean. We spoke to each other in broken English. Consequently, we learned our new language quickly.

Our parents would say, "Oh, just speak Korean to each other."

And we would reply, "We can't; we forgot it," which wasn't strictly true. (Although after a while, it was. To this day, I am far from fluent in my native tongue.) We just wanted to fit in, to become completely Americanized and never think about Korea anymore. The two orphans who were adopted before us, Bob and Teresa, never talked about Korea either. Bob had really bad memories, and Teresa had actually sustained brain damage by banging her head against the wall, as desperate kids do sometimes, to get any kind of stimulation. The two of them had been on the streets in Korea before they were in the orphanage, and they wanted to forget about it.

Our new family gave us presents on the first day. I remember I got my own transistor radio and a G.I. Joe Jeep with a bazooka that actually fired. These brand-new things were *mine*—my first toys. I didn't want to put them down.

EVERYTHING WAS NEW

Even though I was ten years old, my mother used to carry me around like a baby when we first arrived. "It was just too hard to watch you struggle," she recalled. "And you were not very heavy."

Then one day, a neighbor stepped up with some unsolicited advice: "Don't you do that to him. He's intelligent and he'll manage."

That seemed like good advice. She stopped carrying me altogether. Sure enough, I learned how to get around very well, even in the snow and ice of the long Alaskan winter. I did my chores around the house, just like the other kids, and found ways to modify games and outdoor activities so I could participate. My main job became washing the dishes because I could stand in one place to do it.

As soon as winter weather set in, I was surprised when Dad flooded the back yard to make an ice skating rink. There, we would play almost every day, often under outdoor lights. Mom expected us to play outside for at least one hour each day, regardless of the temperature or the short Alaskan days in wintertime. My "skating" consisted of something more like glorified sledding, so I wasn't much of an asset to a hockey team, except as goalie. But I did devise a way to go cross-country skiing with my siblings, and I belonged to the Nordic Ski Club in high school. (I was once voted the Most Inspirational Member for the way I pulled myself along with my arms on my ski-sled.)

With so many boys in the family, we always had a friendly rivalry going, and we would roughhouse all the time, like puppies. My brothers would take advantage of the fact that I couldn't use my legs, but I had a way of getting back at them. I would wait until we were in the back seat of the car together and I was in the middle. Then I would start fights, because there, legs didn't matter.

Winters at the orphanage in South Korea had been damp and cold, so when we first arrived in Alaska, it was hard to believe how fast the temperature plummeted and the snow began to fall. We adjusted quickly. Ice and snow? They don't matter. The house is situated up on a hill? Just get up there. With my braces and crutches, I learned to walk just about everywhere—with great endurance, agility, and speed. I was skinny but strong, and I could carry things in my backpack wherever I went. I wasn't afraid to try new things; I would just forge ahead and do them, always adventuresome and inquisitive.

Back in the orphanage, I had not been able to play many active games. However, I had played marbles for hours in the bare dirt of the enclosure, perfecting my game. When I found out that American kids don't really know how to play marbles, I demonstrated my entrepreneurial talents early by organizing recess marbles tournaments at school—which, given my expertise, I always won handily. With a winner-take-all approach, I not only acquired everyone's marbles, I also turned around and sold them back to the losers so they could play again another day. I was raking in the profits! That is, until my mother started getting phone calls after school from other moms.

"Mrs. Stirling, my son didn't have lunch today because of your Steve."

"What do you mean?"

"He took his lunch money."

Mom sat me down and asked if it was true. I didn't know anyone had used their lunch money to buy back their marbles. So in truth, I did not exactly take anybody's lunch money. But sort of, I did.

"Steve, you have to pay them back."

"But I won fair and square!"

"Maybe so, but you can't make kids buy back their lost marbles!" Reluctantly, I had to comply, sorry to see my good idea go down the drain.

My new American name, Steven Glenn Stirling, was chosen for a special reason: I was named after my father's two best friends, Steve and Glenn. It felt good to have such a thoroughly American name. (Well, Stirling comes from Dad's Scottish roots.) It didn't take long before I felt much more American than I did Korean most of the time.

School was not what I expected. Since we had arrived in August, they enrolled us right away. Eight-year-old Mary Ellen was put into the second grade. I probably should have been put into the fourth grade at that point, but instead I got sent to a special school for the handicapped at about a third-grade level. The first six months were okay because I didn't speak English yet, but after that, I got so bored. They were teaching us two plus two equals four, and my math level was probably a year or two higher than the grade I was supposed to be in. They lumped the physically and mentally challenged kids into the same classroom. That was frustrating because I felt held back by the other kids' limitations. Still, nobody made fun of me—in that school or in any other school for the rest of my education. For the first time in my life, I was accepted on my own merits and I always had lots of friends. Kids *liked* me. It was a big change from Korea. I was kind of a novelty—a Korean kid with crutches.

The school psychologist, a very nice lady named Judith Harkins, felt that handicapped kids should not be integrated into normal classrooms because they might get their feelings hurt and withdraw into themselves. My parents told her, "Well, you don't know Steve very well."

Finally, after about a year, I was mainstreamed into the fourth grade of the regular school, Rabbit Creek Elementary, ending up just one year ahead of my sister. This delayed start would mean that I would be about twenty when I graduated from high school, but it didn't really matter. I reveled in the school environment as much as I delighted in having family to go home to at the end of the day.

Much to her surprise, Mom got pregnant in 1968, two years after we arrived. Baby Earl meant my parents now had seven children. With nine people in that little house on the hill, things got even more congested, but we had a good life together.

HARD-WORKING MOM AND DAD

Words cannot express my appreciation for the way that Mom and Dad worked so hard to make a good home for their big family.

Dad had the same job for thirty years, and we knew we could rely on him. Every workday, he would come home by about 5:30 p.m., just in time for supper with the family. He also limited the number of times he had to travel for work. I always appreciated that. He was there, solid and dependable, every single day. That is really good for family cohesiveness.

It wasn't always easy to give personal attention to so many kids, but he did an especially good job with his four sons. Even though I was adopted later, I was the eldest of them, followed by Dale, Bob, and Earl. Dad taught us how to fish, hunt, and look out for each other. (It was my job to give baths to my little brother Earl. I'm told that one time, he complained that the bath water was too hot. Eager to get the bath over with, I brushed off his concern, saying, "Just blow on it, Earl.") Dad would take us in turns on little fishing trips. He would take my brothers hunting when they got older, but I couldn't go along, except one time, when my job was to post a lookout from the road. Dad did take me on a salmon fishing trip to Seward on Alaska's Kenai Peninsula, just him, his friend, and me.

Needless to say, Mom was a stay-at-home mom. She won Mother of the Year in Alaska in the late 1960s or early '70s, and she deserved the honor for sure. Not only did she do a great job with the seven of us, she also volunteered her time to help take care of babies who were arriving in the States for adoption by others. So did Dad. Sometimes, the planes were only touching down in Anchorage to refuel on their way to someplace else, but the weary caretakers, who always accompanied the children on the long flight across the Pacific Ocean, needed a break. That's where people like Mom came in. She would show up at the airport, relieving the kids' escorts so they get a little rest before they left for Minneapolis or wherever. Mom would change diapers, give bottles to babies, and just do whatever they needed her to do. Sometimes, we kids would come along. We did it for the "Holt babies." One year, Mom received the Molly Holt Award for her volunteerism.

Mom had such a big heart. She was always reaching out to lost animals and kids, especially kids from broken homes. Dad was more cerebral, but he had a big heart, too. The two of them had always gone to church, and they took us to St. John Methodist Church in Anchorage, where we all heard the stories about Jesus. They had us baptized almost as soon as we arrived in the United States. At the same time, typical of their generation, they taught us that all religions take you to God, as if He is the hub, and each religion is a spoke of the wheel. They also felt that good works get you to heaven. Today, I don't agree with everything they taught me about God, but I still think that you couldn't find better people than Jim and Lyn Stirling. They were exemplary parents, honest, loving, and hard-working, who taught us how to cooperate as a team and do our share.

Mom always made plenty of good food, and we never went hungry. We always had meat, vegetables, bread, and seconds. Mom made breakfast for us every day before we went to school and packed lunches for us to take as well. She knew how to stretch a dollar, buying day-old bread, or anything that was on sale, and keeping it in the freezer. Sometimes, when Dad went hunting, he'd get a moose and she'd freeze the meat. In Alaska, wild-caught salmon is standard fare, and we would eat it so often, we got tired of it. We'd say, "Oh, no—salmon for supper again!"

Mom was usually cooking the evening meal when I got home from school and I knew I could always talk with her. "How was your day?" she'd ask, and we'd just chat. At the same time, I would watch her cook, and that's how I learned. Sometimes, I would also help my dad on weekends when he made sourdough pancakes or waffles.

There was always something to look forward to at our house. We'd celebrate the first snow in September with a taffy pull. We'd invite friends over, make different flavors, and take the taffy outside to pull it in the cold until it was stiff. Then we'd spread it out on wax paper, cut it, and wrap it up. Halloween meant parties with homemade costumes. And, of course, we had big celebrations for Thanksgiving, Christmas, and New Year's.

Before Christmas, we would always go out, find our own tree, and cut it down. Christmas was huge at our house because so many of us had been deprived as orphans. Mom and Dad went all out, charging gifts and paying off the bills over the course of the year. They were very generous, and the living room would be filled with presents.

For New Year's dinner, each family member was told to spend about two dollars on some kind of unusual food, like elephant meat or pickled pigs' feet, and everyone was required to at least try everything on the table. Mom would make a main dish, but there would be seven bizarre side dishes.

After Valentine's Day came Easter, with challenging egg hunts because there was still snow on the ground. In fact, looking back, it seems like we always had one celebration or another to look forward to. The end of the school year. Mother's Day. Father's Day. Not to mention all of the birthdays. We had our own talent shows. We even had "Christmas in July" in the summertime, but we gave gifts that we made rather than things we bought at the store. And on the Fourth of July, we'd always drive to nearby Knik Lake and have fun there. With so much going on all the time, we never got bored.

STRONG FAMILY VALUES

I think our family identity was stronger than that of most natural families. The six of us who were adopted knew it, not only the four of us from Korea, but also the two from California. Nobody kept it a secret. Even Patty, who had been adopted as a tiny baby and who looked the most like our parents, knew early on that she was adopted. Dale was five when he was adopted and he'd been in foster care, so he always knew he was adopted. We were an intentional, international family and we just pulled together. Mom always said, "We're a family. We stick together." We might have arguments occasionally, but they always got resolved. We protected our family identity, almost to our detriment. (I noticed much later, after I got married, that I would still side with my family in a controversy rather than with my wife. I'd had it drilled into me that the family was always the first consideration, and I guess it took me a while to consider my wife as part of my family.)

As a Korean adopted by Caucasian parents, I thought of myself as white, which is why kids like me are called "Twinkies" or "bananas"—yellow on the outside, white on the inside. When I first came to Alaska, I used to make fun of Korean people all the time. When other kids would say, "Wait a minute, aren't you Korean?" I'd say, "No, I'm not Korean. I'm Scottish."

Four adopted Korean kids growing up in the same Alaskan family was unusual enough that discrimination was unheard-of. We were definitely a novelty. To this day, I don't fit in when I'm with Korean people because I can't speak the language. And when I'm with Caucasians, I don't fit in because I don't look the same. But when I'm with Christians, those differences disappear, because no matter what our skin color, we're all related by the blood of Jesus Christ.

With so many kids, we had arguments and fights, but overall, things were very stable. We knew what it meant to be loved unconditionally. We found it easy to accept our parents' values, one of which they stated often: "Help make this world a better place before you leave." This foundation contributed greatly to my own choices in life.

BECOMING NATURALIZED CITIZENS

After about two years, Mary Ellen and I became naturalized citizens. We were ten and twelve years old. Bob and Teresa were already citizens by that time. It's much easier for kids than it is for adults because kids don't have to take an exam first. In fact, we didn't really realize what we were doing. We just "got naturalized." We each received a little American flag and a copy of a congratulatory letter from our senators. That was it. Only fairly recently have I considered what it means, in depth, to become naturalized because I was asked to give the keynote speech at a local naturalization ceremony in Brunswick, Georgia. I spoke about taking on your responsibilities as a citizen, contributing in a positive way, and thinking first of the United States rather than your native country.

I distinctly remember when Mom told all of her Korean kids matter-of-factly, not trying to scare us, "When you become a naturalized citizen of the United States, you are free to do a lot of things. But you will never be allowed to become the president of the United States because you weren't born here. Just be sure not to do something really bad. Then you might get deported."

That was a new word. "What's 'deported'?"

"Well," she said, "it means they can send you back to your native country."

I asked, "You mean like on vacation?"

"No, I mean like forever."

What?! "You mean they could send me back to Korea for being bad?"

"Yes, but you'd have to be *really* bad."

I'm not going to do anything bad, then, I vowed silently. *I will be the best kid they ever saw. I do not want to go back to Korea.*

Therefore, I ended up working really hard at everything I did. Some of it was just because I didn't want to disappoint my mom and dad, and make them sorry that they had adopted me. Some of it was because I felt I needed to prove I was just as good as someone who was not disabled. But some of it, at first anyway, was so I would not get deported. What a strong motivation that misconception provided!

STILL HAD MORE MISADVENTURES

I had always been fairly mischievous back in the orphanage. That did not go away when I moved to Alaska. For example, there was the infamous "tongue incident." If you have seen the movie *A Christmas Story*, you will recall the scene where one kid triple-dog-dares another to put his wet tongue on an icy metal flagpole.[6] Well, one of us dared the others to imitate that. (I won't say it couldn't have been me.) Our house had long metal railings next to the steps that led up to the front porch. It was freezing weather. Before long, six Stirling kids, all in a row, were trapped with their tongues frozen to the railing. (Lucky for Earl, he was still a baby, so he was inside the house.) We yelled, "Gaah! Awwgh! Maaa!!" Mom came outside, laughing so hard she could hardly get a pot of hot coffee and pour it down the railing to get our tongues unstuck. We never did that again.

A DIFFERENT KIND OF PAIN

My parents were concerned about what kind of painful post-polio surgery I might need. My mom met with an orthopedic surgeon who had served in the military in Korea, and he assured her, "Oh, Mrs. Stirling, you won't have to worry about it because the Koreans can't feel pain." He must have treated only tough-as-rocks Korean soldiers.

Fortunately, my parents looked for another doctor.

Over time, I had many surgeries on my legs at the nearby hospital in Anchorage. Then when I was in ninth grade, old enough to have almost finished growing, I had to go to the Shriners Hospital in Portland, Oregon, for a major back surgery. (The Shriners pay for everything so that kids whose parents can't afford it can get operations they need. Also, they have the best-qualified orthopedic surgeons.) They implanted

---

6. *A Christmas Story*, directed by Bob Clark (1983; MGM/UA Entertainment Co.).

stainless steel "Harrington rods" next to my spinal column to hold it straighter.

I finished ninth grade while I was recuperating in the hospital. For the first five months, I was really a good patient. Then I got bored.

My bed was in a big room with other boys twelve to fifteen years old. They had different capabilities because they were there for different reasons. So I would get other kids to do things for me because I couldn't get out of bed. Once, I got them to string together all of our water bottles and urinals all the way around the room, and put the end of the string across the door. Then someone called out, "Nurse!" When the nurse opened the double doors, the string got tugged and everything spilled, all over the room, domino-style.

"Whose idea was that?" she demanded.

"Mine," I admitted.

"Okay, you're grounded." And to enforce that, she said, "Since you acted like a little kid, that's where we'll put you." So they moved my bed into the room with the five- and six-year-olds. I didn't let another chance go by. I got my harmonica and started to play it really loud, waking up all the kids.

"Okay, troublemaker," they said, "We're putting you back in the junior high room."

We would use our drinking straws to shoot spitballs way high onto the ceiling. The place was old with a very high ceiling, so when spitballs got stuck, they were up there for good, totally out of reach.

I remember a stretch of time when people from a church used to come regularly into the ward to share the gospel. They always seemed to come right at the time when we wanted to watch *Star Trek*. We wanted to watch TV more than we wanted to listen to them! So when one guy asked, "Do you want to accept Christ?" I said, "Yeah, I'll accept Christ," thinking to myself, *because I want to watch Star Trek!* "Now can I watch my show?" When he came again the next week at the same time, it was too much. I told him, "Listen, I accepted Christ last week. Do I have to listen to the gospel *again?*"

Eventually, I graduated from the bed to a wheelchair. One day, another kid impressed me by popping a wheelie with his wheelchair. I decided to try it myself. But I didn't realize that you have to hold onto the wheels when you do it to keep the wheelchair from going backward. So I toppled over. I didn't get hurt because the handlebar hit the ground first, but the nurse was furious at me for attempting something so foolish.

That hospital became a very special place for me because it was the only place I could have received that much-needed back surgery. Someday, I'll go back and visit.

MISSING KOREAN FOOD, ESPECIALLY KIMCHI

With four Korean-Americans in the family, it should come as no surprise that we loved Korean food. But in Alaska in the 1960s and '70s, Korean food was hard to find. There were no Korean grocery stores or restaurants, so Mom had to do her best with what she had. The national dish of Korea is *kimchi*—spicy, fermented, pickled vegetables. The napa cabbage could be flown in from California, but the dish calls for a combination of spices and flavorings that we couldn't get easily. The best Mom could do was to take sauerkraut and mix hot red pepper into it!

That's why, when my brother Bob was a teenager, he introduced himself to Douglas An, a fellow Korean and the brother of my future wife. Right away, Bob asked, "Can your mom make kimchi?"

"Of *course* she can. She's Korean."

After we met the An family, they became our source of kimchi. When they gave some to us, we'd finish the entire jar in one day.

GIRLS AND CARS

Like any red-blooded teenage boy, I liked girls. Mostly, they liked me back. Well, not the girl I liked in elementary school. I expressed my admiration for her by poking her bottom with my crutch and leaving a dirty bull's-eye mark. She decided I needed to be taught a lesson, so she pushed me hard and knocked me over. I could hear the bone in my leg break, and the pain was excruciating. "Never mind," said the doctor when he looked at the X-ray. It will heal." That leg was already in a cast because of some polio-related surgery. The girl was remorseful, and I never put crutch marks on her again.

To give me some independence, my dad did some research and found out about a company that made hand controls for cars so that paraplegics could learn to drive. Because he was an engineer, he installed those controls on our old 1964 Chevy Impala station wagon, and when I was sixteen, I got my license. Now I could go anywhere, and it was thrilling. I might not be able to walk fast or swim fast, but now, I could *drive* fast.

To teach me how to use the controls, Dad had to learn how to use them himself. With these controls, you steer with one hand; with the other, you push in for the brakes and down for the gas, using a little toggle switch for the high-beam headlights. The hand controls could be moved from one car to the next, and I used them up until I went off to college, when I didn't have a car. To this day, I can drive just about any vehicle if I can install my hand controls in it.

I got a job as a cashier at the Oriental Gardens, saved up $1,000, and bought a 1967 GTO, the car known as "the goat." It was a hot car, red with a white top. It had a 386 Hurst shift on it, and it was so powerful that in the wintertime, it would just spin out. With hand controls, just a little push really hits the gas or the brakes hard, and it's tough to get the feel of the pedals that way. I ended up in a lot of ditches, despite the load of sand I put in the trunk to add extra weight.

One time, I wanted to impress a girl, so I asked her if I could pick her up and drive her to school. I had her with me in the car, and I decided to pass a slow school bus. Bad idea. I accelerated, and we hit an icy patch and spun out into the ditch. We weren't hurt because there was so much snow everywhere, but that girl never rode with me again.

Eventually, I sold that car and bought a Vega, which was the complete opposite of the GTO. It had good gas mileage and a little engine. It didn't have *enough* power. I was driving it when I was going to take my SATs, running a little late. I pushed too hard and ended up going off the road—only that time, I somehow skidded right back onto the road.

What a combination: a foolhardy kid driving with hand controls under Alaskan road conditions! God saved me multiple times.

Not that it was always the road's fault. One time, our family was involved with summer swim meets, and my dad asked me to go down to the corner A&W to get some change, so I jumped in the car and went. It wasn't far, and a friend of ours owned the place. Steering with my one hand made power steering a must because when I turned the wheel, I'd have to let it straighten itself out. I whirled into the A&W driveway and failed to allow enough time for the wheel to straighten out. Wham! I hit the cement-block wall of the establishment. The bumper and the side of the car were dented up, but it was drivable.

The store owner came out. "Oh. Hi, Steve."

Dad and I went back later and repaired the concrete and repainted it. But Dad wanted me to learn how to get the car repaired, so he told me to arrange the body work. I looked in the phone book and called a place called The Body Shop. A sweet woman answered, "Hello-ooo."

"Hi," I said, "Do you guys work on Chevys?"

"No, we don't, you smart aleck!" *Click.* (It was not one of *those* body shops.)

DRIVEN TO ACCOMPLISH ANYTHING

I was pretty intense about everything. I might not have been capable of running in track meets or playing on the ice hockey team, but I could apply myself diligently to any task that involved my mind or my hands. I couldn't dig ditches, but I could use my brain. I could overachieve.

I was outgoing and energetic, and I just liked to do things. Many times, I would launch into action without thinking, but I was resourceful, too, even creative, at least when it came to trying something new or selling something (like marbles). I liked the idea of earning money. Being an ambitious, driven young man has its plusses because you can achieve great things. But it has its minuses, too, as I found out over time.

One downside was that I could never admit I was wrong. This fault plagued me for decades and interfered with many significant relationships, particularly my marriage. But the problem began much earlier than that.

When my mom was trying to teach me how to write my name, "Steve," in cursive, she said, "You write the whole name and then you come back and cross the *t*."

"No," I insisted. "I write the *S* and the *t*, then I stop and cross it. Then I complete the rest."

"No, you cross the *t* at the end."

"No." I stubbornly put down the pencil and refused to write at all.

"Steve, listen to me…" Back and forth we went.

Finally, she got so frustrated, she batted me with her hand. What a shock! My mother had *hit* me. "Now do it right!"

I relented. "Okay."

I liked to have control and I began to plan everything. That tendency may be helpful for being a manager or executive, but only if it's balanced. When life flowed with my plan, I was happy. If things didn't go according to my plan, I got upset.

On the plus side, I was not very inward-directed or self-protective. I didn't want others to feel uncomfortable around me because of my disability. So I just opened up to people, and they usually responded positively. My personality helped me rise above distractions and just get things done.

Selling things suited me well. I was never afraid to ask someone to buy candy or whatever to support the school band. (I played first trumpet in the ninth-grade band when I was still in seventh grade because I practiced so much. I also taught myself how to play the guitar when I was in the Shriners hospital.)

While the other kids were outside playing, I would always say, "I'm gonna study. I want to get ahead."

One day, I asked my parents, "What are the best colleges in the United States?"

"Well," they replied, "the Ivy League schools and Stanford."

"I'm going to one of them," I declared.

"Steve, we want you kids to go to college, but you know we cannot afford to send all of you to expensive private schools," they said. Seven kids would cost too much, even at inexpensive colleges.

So I began to work hard to achieve my goal, and my diligence paid off.

5

POMP AND CIRCUMSTANCE

Am I now trying to win the approval of human beings, or of God? Or am I trying to please people? If I were still trying to please people, I would not be a servant of Christ.
—Galatians 1:10 (NIV)

Once I decided I was going to work to get accepted at one of the premier universities in the country, I would not let anything deflect me from reaching that goal. I was already working hard in school, but I would need scholarships, too. "I really want to go to one of the best schools," I told my parents.

But they were realists. They told me, "Steve, those schools are very expensive. Also, they are very hard to get into"—which was a nice way of saying, "You're not *that* smart," which I wasn't. Still, I just knew that God would provide because I had told Him many times about my dreams for the future.

I laid out a strategy for my last couple of years in high school. I would get good grades. I would look for summer jobs where I could both earn money and improve my business-related skills, such as accounting. I would step up my involvement in leadership-building activities. And I would enjoy high school life to the fullest.

Studying always came first. Two of my brothers didn't need to study in order to get good grades, but I did. Much of the time, I chose to forego after-school fun in order to hit the books. Not that I was a total bookworm. I had lots of friends. I went to parties. I won citizenship awards. I got involved in student government and found other ways to meet people. In my junior year, I ran for class president and won. This opened new doors for me. It was the first time a Korean-American had ever been class president at Service High School and also the first time a disabled student had won any office.

The Anchorage school board oversees a number of high schools. In my senior year, I was selected by my fellow area high school student body presidents to represent them on the school board. In turn, the board sent me to attend a national convention of student body presidents in Atlanta, Georgia, which was an honor and gave me a glimpse of my future life. (Little did I suspect then that I would someday live and work in Atlanta.)

More than I could have realized at the time, every new activity and role was helping to prepare me for the future. When I had to get up in front of groups to give speeches, I discovered that I was much too nervous, so I joined Toastmasters. They coached me and gave me chances to practice new skills. (Later in life, speaking experience led naturally to leadership in Rotary International, and it equipped me to share both the gospel and my personal testimony in many settings, such as Bible study fellowship groups.)

I applied for and won the first of several scholarships that helped me attend the University of Alaska Anchorage (UAA). I had decided to go there first to get my prerequisites out of the way and still live at home, thus saving money.

At last, the day of my high school graduation arrived. As I walked forward with the rest of my classmates to receive my diploma, the school band played the piece of music that we always hear at graduations, "Pomp and Circumstance." Most of us don't realize that the tune has words. It started out as a military march in Great Britain, where it is known as "Land of Hope and Glory." Lyrics were added for the coronation of King Edward VII in 1901. Subsequently, the music was played in composer Edward Elgar's honor when he came to the United States to receive an honorary degree at Yale, whereupon it took off as a popular graduation song.[7]

As the music played, it reflected my personal pomp and circumstance; my ambitions and hard work had only begun to pay off. Even though I was more inclined to give myself the credit than God, I didn't realize that He was engineering everything in my life, both defeats and victories, for His glory. I never could have dreamed how my life would turn out. He had heard me back when I had cried out to Him from my sleeping mat on the orphanage floor, and He was turning all of my liabilities into advantages.

DISCOVERING NEW HORIZONS

The summer after graduation was filled with new adventures. With my brothers Dale and Bob, I went on a seven-day sailing trip on Prince William Sound east of Anchorage, starting out from Whittier, Alaska. The trip was a graduation present from our parents. We were in a twenty-two-foot sailboat following our guide, who sailed in another

7. The title "Pomp and Circumstance" comes from a line spoken by Shakespeare's *Othello*, "Pride, pomp, and circumstance of glorious war!" The key ideas of pride and expanding boundaries fit well with the whole idea of graduation. In this country, we have discarded the war connotations.

boat with his wife and daughter. What a stunning way to see that part of God's amazing creation! Even taking a bath was an adventure; my method involved soaping up with dishwashing detergent and then taking a swim in the ice-cold water with a huge glacier in the distance.

That summer, I also went with my high school friends Jon Ah You and Richard Welsh on a canoe trip that involved lots of portaging. We would paddle for hours, and when we came to an area where we couldn't canoe, they would carry the canoe and backpacks while I traversed the rough terrain with my crutches. It was such an exhausting trip that we didn't even have the energy to put up a tent at night; we just slept under the stars next to our campfire's embers. Once, we were thrilled to see a newborn baby moose.

These were exciting, incomparable experiences, and they provided me with fond memories as I went off to more urban adventures.

ENTER THE BEAUTIFUL SOOK HEE

Kyung Yon An, the woman who made kimchi for us Korean Stirlings, and her husband, Byung Joo An, had a beautiful daughter named Sook Hee. I had my eye on her after meeting her at a Korean picnic in high school.

I'd never had much luck in the dating department. Although I had plenty of friends who were girls, I had never had an actual girlfriend. All the way through high school, I would develop crushes, then get my heart broken, repeatedly. As a result, my prayers had started taking a different form. Instead of asking for a girlfriend first, I started to ask God for a *wife*. My consistent prayer was this one: "Father, would You make her kind, would You make her gentle, would You make her wise? And, since You're the God of the Universe, on top of that, would You please make her beautiful?"

In a ploy to get to know Sook Hee better, I asked her to tutor me in Korean. I did it more for the sake of wanting to get her attention and spend time with her than for relearning Korean. I did want to be able at least to write in Korean, but I didn't really care about learning to speak it again. We had periodic Korean lessons for about a year while we were both attending the University of Alaska.

Her family had emigrated from Korea when she was sixteen, coming to Anchorage because her aunt had married an American G.I., was living there already, and invited them. Sook Hee had jumped into school and the social scene right away, and her family had high hopes for her. I knew for a fact that their high hopes did not include a Korean orphan with polio—the worst kind of husband material in the eyes of any traditional Korean parent. But I was used to hoping against hope and reaching for the stars.

RECEIVING HELP FROM ALL CORNERS

My goal of attending an Ivy League university was like reaching for the stars, too, and I could not have attempted it without the help of others. My parents continued to be supportive of my every effort, and I did live at home for the first two years of college at UAA. I majored in accounting, with the idea that it would provide me with steady employment. Scholarships helped greatly: National Certified Public Accountant and Alaskan of the Year scholarships, along with one from Daughters of the American Revolution.

I enjoyed accounting…up to a point. But the more I got into it, the more I realized that all of those rules and stipulations did not match my personality. The intermediate level of accounting is what usually separates true accountants from the rest. When I hit that point, I could see that I was losing my enthusiasm for accounting. However, I knew I could still use it for a springboard. What I really liked to do was sell things. I started to think that an applied business major would be a better choice.

When it came time to apply to transfer to another university, I still wanted to try for one of the Ivy League schools. So I decided to apply to all eight of them in order to have a better chance of getting into one. I had saved up enough money to pay for the application fees, but I was not the world's best typist. Golda Whitaker, a dear family friend who worked as the school secretary at Rabbit Creek Elementary, stepped in to help. Each of those eight complicated applications had to be typed perfectly in duplicate, using carbon paper. I could supply the words to fill in the blanks, but I couldn't prepare all of those applications single-handedly. Thank you, Mrs. Whitaker!

I was not surprised when most of the schools said no. But two of them, Cornell and Wharton, wrote back that, yes, I could come as a transfer student. Both of them, however, required some additional prerequisites. The Wharton School at the University of Pennsylvania wanted me to repeat a whole year of the accounting classes I had just completed at UAA. But Cornell told me I only had to take two additional classes beforehand. I didn't want to lose a whole year, so I chose Cornell and did the required coursework at the UAA summer school while I kept up with my full-time job working in the accounting department at Sohio/BP so that I could pay for my plane ticket to New York. Student loans and a scholarship from the state of Alaska would pay for everything else.

KNOW NO ONE? NO PROBLEM!

Ithaca, New York, is a long way from Anchorage, Alaska, and I didn't know a soul there. No problem. True to my "just do it" nature, I just took off on Allegheny Airlines, along with another guy from

Anchorage who was going to be a freshman. After I got there, I would figure out where to live and how to get around.

We got there very late and found a place to sleep in the school gym. I couldn't find my toothpaste in the dark, so my friend loaned me his. That stuff tasted terrible. Next morning, the light of day showed me that I had brushed my teeth with his Brylcreem. That was only a humorous inconvenience compared to the much bigger challenges I would have to conquer in my new city.

Cornell did not have an undergraduate business degree program, so I enrolled in their agricultural economics program, which offers an applied business curriculum. I opted to live in a high-rise dorm on the university's north campus, and I took a ten-cent bus ride to the main campus every day. I walked everywhere wearing my heavy backpack and made friends with other transfer students. I am still friends with my suite-mates from those two years. I didn't go to church or read the Bible, but I did continue to talk to God on my own.

That first winter in 1978 was challenging for students like me because it included an Alaskan amount of snow and freezing temperatures. It was really hard to get around and keep up with the workload, but I persisted and never missed any classes. No excuses were allowed, including being on crutches.

For about a year, I was privileged to serve on Cornell's "504 committee," the team working to make the campus compliant with the federal Rehabilitation Act of 1973. Section 504 of the act prohibits discrimination based on disability in the student population. Our committee recommended changes that would make attending class more manageable for students with disabilities.

I was driven. I wanted to go straight from Cornell to get my MBA someplace. "Someplace" turned out to be one of the finest business schools in the country: the Kellogg Graduate School of Management at Northwestern University in Evanston, Illinois, just outside Chicago. When I was accepted, I began to feel that I could do anything I set my mind to. While the other students were partying, I studied. I hardly ever drank or went to parties. I had a poster in my room that reminded me: "Happy are those who dream dreams—and are willing to pay the price to make them come true."

When I graduated from Cornell in 1980 with my B.S. in Agricultural Economics, it was such a big deal that my whole family flew down from Alaska to attend the ceremony. Afterward, one of my best friends from Cornell, Johnny Fung, gave them their first tour of New York City and our first taste of dim sum, which they remember to this day.[8] My world was expanding rapidly.

OPEN DOORS AT NORTHWESTERN

In what was surely an answer to prayer, I had received a full leadership scholarship (for minorities) from Johnson & Johnson to attend the Kellogg Graduate School of Management (KGSM) at Northwestern. I set off for the state of Illinois.

During my first year, I served as a student representative on the KGSM admissions committee. On Wednesdays, we would read through all of the applications and decide which people to admit to the school. Being behind the scenes like that made me realize how truly extraordinary it was for me to have been accepted there myself, and at Cornell before that. Clearly, God was guiding my life and opening doors for me. "*With God all things are possible*" (Matthew 19:26 NIV).

Still, I was much too busy with graduate school to acknowledge God much. The very next year, I was selected to study international business

---

8. My biological father died in Korea that same year, although I didn't know that until much later.

in France at the prestigious École Supérieure des Sciences Economiques et Commerciales (ESSEC)—one of the top business schools in Europe. A suburb of Paris, Cergy-Pontoise, France, would become my address for the next four months.

I had studied French in junior high, high school, and college for a couple of years. Still, I needed more help to learn how to conduct my daily affairs in French, not to mention how to understand what was going on in class. I arrived three weeks before classes started so I could take intensive French lessons every day.

My good friend from high school, Richard, had been accepted into a program in Germany at the same time. For one semester after he finished, Richard, my friend Bruce Kelm from Kellogg, and I got a one-bedroom apartment together. We hosted international parties where we would sing, and I would play the guitar. Our French friend, Jacques Brial, still has a recording of my playing from one of those sessions.

When in France, you must do as the French do. That includes drinking wine. Unfortunately, that got me into a few unusual situations. Once, we invited this six-foot-tall French teenager over for dinner at our apartment. He happened to have a prosthetic leg, which affected his gait. After a dinner that included a fair amount of wine, he was tipsy and so was I. He needed help to walk down the street to make a phone call, and he decided to hang onto *me* for support. We must have made quite a comical-looking pair. It would not have been easy to get back up if we had taken a fall together.

Another time, Richard and I were in Amsterdam and went to a Chinese restaurant. Afterward, we thought we'd get a beer someplace nearby. Conveniently, there was a place almost next door, so we went in. We didn't realize it was a topless bar. We paid a modest cover charge and it seemed like a comfortable place. When two of the topless waitresses came over, we should have said, "We'll just finish our beers and go," but they persuaded us to buy them a bottle of champagne. I thought they said it would be about $7.00, which seemed like a good deal, so I agreed. Before the four of us had finished that bottle, the girls said they wanted another. The maître-d' told me this next bottle was much better than the first one. "How much was the first bottle?" I asked. "$75.00." We'd been *had*.

The girls took off. Richard and I took turns going into the men's room, hiding most of our money in our shoes and socks. Then when the inevitable happened—the owner coming over and demanding payment, asking, "How much money do you have?"—we could pull out our wallets and display only about $45.00 total. We surrendered that amount and got out of there as fast as we could, in one piece. Lesson learned.

BUT SIR, THIS IS PARIS!

At ESSEC, we would attend classes from Monday through Thursday and then we would have long weekends for traveling on our Eurail passes. Once we had a whole week off. We went to Pamplona for the running of the bulls. We went to Madrid, Toledo, Barcelona, Granada, Venice—everywhere.

Early on, I persuaded my sister Patty, then a high school senior, to visit me. She flew to London, where I met her, and we stayed with one of our mother's friends from high school. We took the ferry across to France. I couldn't carry my own bags, so she had to carry everything. The crossing was kind of rough, and there were lots of stairs. After we got off the boat, we took a train and then a subway to get into Paris. We were exhausted. We decided to go to the first hotel we saw, which was a pretty expensive one. "I'll pay for it on my credit card," I said. "Let's just stay right here." We entered the impressive lobby, and I spoke to the desk clerk in French: "Monsieur, je voudrais une chambre avec deux lits." ("Sir, I would like one room with two beds.")

He raised his eyebrow. "Monsieur, pourquoi?" He glanced at my sister—very cute, blonde hair. "Sir, we will give you *one* bed..."

"Non. Une chambre avec *deux* lits, s'il vous plait!"

"Mais monsieur, c'est Paris. You do not have to worry about anything."

Then I said, "She's really my sister." All of the staff started to laugh. "No, really! She *is* my sister."

Finally he relented. He was so disappointed.

After seeing Paris, Patty and I decided to "drop in" on Richard, who was just finishing up his studies in Munich. So without notifying him, we figured out on our own how to take the train and then a taxi to his address. When we knocked on the door and he opened it, he couldn't believe his eyes. He took us to Oktoberfest, and then for the next two weeks, we traveled together, visiting Venice, Italy, and the French Riviera. In Nice, we rented a sailboat and had some adventures, such as the time I went for a midnight swim by myself, and the strong current took me out to sea. I only got back safely by swimming parallel to the shore for a long time. At the end of our time together, Patty flew back to Anchorage to finish her senior year.

On one long weekend, Richard and I went to visit Le Mont-Saint-Michel, the famous mountain-island with its ancient abbey on the coast of Normandy. It's a long walk from the train station across the flat approach at low tide, especially with crutches and a backpack. Then we found a tour group with whom we could climb up the mountain by stair steps...with no railings. I managed to keep up with everyone. But when we got into the medieval Mont Saint Michel Abbey at the top, and I saw that the descent down involved a steep spiral staircase, I told Richard to go on without me; I would just wait there for him to come back up. It was a nice room in the sky, with old windows all around.

I waited and enjoyed the spectacular view. Waited some more and wondered what was taking so long. Waited and looked around and noticed that nobody had come through any of the doorways in a long time. Finally I thought, *Well, I'd better go back down the way I came up.* But the door was locked! I banged on the door: "Let me out!" I was a prisoner in the tower room. "God, if you get me out of here, I'll go to church!"

Finally, after I had banged on the door for a long time, someone came and unlocked it. As it turned out, every tour was supposed to just pass through that room at the top and descend by the spiral staircase, and an attendant would always lock the door behind the group. When Richard figured out what had happened, they sent someone up for me. Whew! We took it in stride (weak pun intended).

SHE WORE A PURPLE FRENCH BERET...

In the midst of all of my international travel, I had forgotten Sook Hee. When my semester at ESSEC was over at the end of 1981, I flew back to Anchorage for the holidays. One gray day, my mom asked me to go to the mall to do some Christmas shopping.

Walking down the big hallway, I spotted Sook Hee with her parents. I hadn't seen her in four years, and she looked spectacular, wearing a purple wool French beret at a jaunty angle. Her smile lit up the mall. She had come with her parents to shop and translate for them.

Fresh from my travels overseas, I blurted out, "I have a question for you, Sook Hee.... Do you know how they kiss in France?" Sook Hee shook her head.

Disregarding the presence of her parents and their Korean reserve about public displays of affection, I spontaneously stretched up to reach her face and planted kisses on both cheeks, which immediately turned red with embarrassment.

At least I only kissed her on her cheeks, but that was bad enough. Mr. An said something in Korean, and they hurried off. *Well, that was awkward,* I mused as I collected myself. *Dumb. Way to go, Steve.*

During Christmas week, I invited Sook Hee twice to our home, but we were never alone together. Then on New Year's Day, I invited myself over to visit her family again. They all expected our whole family to come. But having told my family that they had invited me by myself, I showed up alone. At the end of the evening, Sook Hee had to give me a ride home, and I gave her a second kiss—on the forehead.

Was she getting interested in me now? When it was time for me to fly back to Northwestern, she told her parents that she was going to the Anchorage airport to say good-bye to her cousin Larry as he returned to the University of Washington. Only later did she tell me that the real reason was to see me off.

From Illinois, I started writing letters and phoning her. Mrs. An told her daughter, "It seems like he's getting serious. But you can't get serious with him." Left unspoken was the Korean cultural opposition to having a romantic relationship with an orphan or a cripple. "You don't want to hurt him by getting serious with him and then breaking it off. What are you going to do about it?"

"Well," said Sook Hee with a little smile, "if he asks me to marry him, I will marry him!"

6

NEW LIFE SAGA

From the beginning of the creation, God "made them male and female. For this reason a man shall leave his father and mother and be joined to his wife, and the two shall become one flesh"; so then they are no longer two, but one flesh.
—Mark 10:6–8

Ever the high achiever, I carried my personal ten-year plan on a small piece of folded paper in my wallet so I could keep my goals in the forefront of my mind. I looked at it often. First on the list: I needed to finish my MBA at KGSM. The school was fast-tracking me, and I knew I would be offered a good job. On that assumption, my second goal was to save up at least $30,000 within two years after graduation. Then, and only then, I would ask some woman to marry me. My future wife wouldn't have to be Korean, but I figured she probably would be. (I wasn't deterred by those prejudices among Koreans about eligible women marrying handicapped orphans—nor by the fact that I would probably be too busy to have a social life.) Then, even before the ten years were up, my plan predicted that my beautiful bride and I would launch our life. We would live the American dream. We would buy the perfect house and make more money each year as I climbed the rungs of the corporate ladder. It was going to be great.

However, there was nothing written in the plan about a beautiful Korean girl wearing a purple French beret. Something had changed during that short week at Christmas. Now I couldn't get Sook Hee out of my mind and heart. Later on, I would make the connection between what happened and my earlier prayers, in which I had skipped to the chase and asked God for a wife instead of a girlfriend.

It was beginning to look as though I would need some more of that brash energy so I could make a big modification to my well-considered ten-year plan.

STRAIGHT TO THE FINISH

Back at Northwestern after Christmas, I plunged into my second year. I discovered I really liked marketing classes. I enjoyed learning how to promote, advertise, and sell things. I liked knowing about forecasts. I relished all of the aspects of figuring out how to run the marketing side of a business.

It was a high privilege to have won the Johnson & Johnson leadership award that was paying my way at Northwestern, which I had applied for back when I was still at Cornell. Quite a few people applied, and we all had to be interviewed individually. The committee was very selective as they narrowed the field down to about ten people. This represented a big investment on their part, and they didn't want to waste it. The scholarship would pay for MBA tuition at certain schools, and it would also include work during the summer, kind of like a paid internship. They paid me about $3,000 a month, which was a lot of money back in 1980. That took care of my room and board. It was a very generous deal that I am still grateful for today. The internship also allowed the people at Johnson & Johnson to observe candidates in the field to help them decide whether to invite the interns to continue with the company after graduation. I could have interned with a focus on finance, but that all changed when I met Wayne Nelson, who was then the president of the division I was working for, McNeil Consumer Products Company.[9] Wayne thought my background and interests made me better suited to marketing, and he knew what he was talking about. So marketing it was. My advisor at Cornell, Dr. Dana Goodrich, had also recommended that I go into marketing.

Besides learning about marketing for business, I stepped up my efforts to market myself to a certain beautiful girl back in Anchorage. I wrote more letters in the following two months than I have ever written in my life, before or since. But since my handwriting is so hard to decipher, I had to make many phone calls, too—to tell Sook Hee what the letters said. As the weeks turned into months, my feelings for her were growing, along with my phone bill.

CAUTION: HANDLE WITH CARE

Sook Hee's feelings were growing, too. She probably had a better idea than I did about what to look for in a potential mate because she had dated so much. In fact, she had just broken an engagement to marry a well-educated Korean man, although her family had considered him an ideal match.

What would make an ideal match in their eyes? A man with prospects for a prosperous future—a man who was well brought up, well-educated, intelligent, healthy, and strong. There were not many Koreans at that time who fit that description. Orphans started out with a handicap even if they did not have crippled legs as I did. Through no fault of their own, they carry the misfortune of having a sketchy background. As a

9. Later, Wayne Nelson became well-known as the founder of Nelson Communications, a group of specialized pharmaceutical service companies.

result, they may grow up to be depressed and angry. Seldom do they have any money. They may have been abused and not know how to love because they had nobody to teach them. They may betray you because they were betrayed. They are unpredictable because their background is unknown, a blank. Koreans were particularly cautious about allowing people into their lives about whose background they knew so little, lest they bring trouble.

Sook Hee could have moved back to Korea, where she would have lived like a queen by entering into an arranged marriage, but she had not wanted to do that. Korean people had started coming to America in greater numbers in the late 1960s, and Sook Hee had moved to the States with her parents and brother in November 1971 because they wanted to have greater opportunities than they could find back in Korea. She didn't necessarily want to stay in Alaska for the rest of her life, but she wanted to stay in the United States.

The "orphan" label had not deterred Sook Hee from anyone she had dated up until that time. She had dated orphans from both Korea and China. One guy had escaped from China with his sister, and they had fled to Hong Kong, leaving their parents behind. They were not true orphans any more than I was, but they had kind of raised themselves.

Even Sook Hee's father was an orphan and so was her grandfather. In some ways, that particular taboo was weaker in their family. But there was still a problem when it came to physical handicaps. Where I was concerned, that factor loomed large in her parents' minds. Also, we found out later that her aunt and uncle in Anchorage, who thought of Sook Hee almost as a daughter, had seen me years before she ever came to America, when I must have been scooting around on the floor instead of using crutches. That gave her uncle the strong negative impression that any woman who married me would be doomed to take care of me for the rest of her life because I was so severely handicapped.

IN NEED OF KISSING LESSONS

My kissing Sook Hee in the middle of the mall in front of her parents certainly did not improve their impression of me. Korean parents tend to be very protective and conservative. They had allowed Sook Hee to date a lot—in fact, she says she may have dated as many as fifty different guys after high school—but she didn't get very intimate with any of them. As she says, "I was comfortable around guys. I had a brother. In Korea, my father drove a taxi and my mother used to have a room and board business in our home. Most of the guests were males. Therefore, I had grown up surrounded by males. When I started dating after high school, I went out with almost any guy who invited me. But as soon as a date wanted to get serious, I just said bye!"

Mr. An always stayed up late until she came home from her dates in the evening. No one had ever dared to kiss Sook Hee in front of her parents.

Everything in her upbringing had been super-conservative. She had attended a girls' school in Busan, Korea, where she grew up, where they had strict rules about being with the opposite sex. The school atmosphere was so carefully controlled that if they ever showed a movie that contained a kissing scene, it would always be cut out because kissing was considered too sexual. Yet Sook Hee had a romantic side, like most girls.

She was quickly finding out that I was the kind of guy who acts first and thinks later. She says she would have been even more embarrassed if she had known what a "French kiss" really is—which obviously didn't occur to me before the words, "Do you know how they kiss in France?" came out of my mouth. At least her lack of awareness sheltered her a little bit from my inappropriate question!

Sook Hee and I did not find out until later that we were both born on February 24, just one year apart. But whereas I had been abandoned early by my parents, she had always been closely guarded by hers. And although our families had become friends in Alaska, Sook Hee says she doesn't remember meeting me at the Korean picnic. However, she can understand why my family might remember her. Apparently, she was the only girl there who had long hair, which would have made her stand out. Also, I remember returning from that picnic and hearing Mom say, "Wouldn't it be wonderful if Sook Hee would be your wife someday!" In other words, while the Ans did not consider me husband material, for eight or ten years, my mom had been hoping that Sook Hee would become her daughter-in-law.

GETTING TO KNOW EACH OTHER

In Korea, Sook Hee had always been a pretty good student, but she was a loner both by choice and because of Mrs. An's strict rules. Many ordinary and harmless experiences were forbidden to her. In many ways, her family life was quite stable, but because of parental harshness and the overall dynamics of the relationships between family members, she characterizes it as "dysfunctional." She worked hard to become closer to her mother, and it has paid off as tensions have eased over the years.

Moving the whole family from Korea to Anchorage, Alaska, must have marked an enormous change for everyone. Sook Hee was in the middle of her high school years, and her parents had made the big move in part for the sake of her education. Thus, even more was now expected of her. She put her energy into learning English and studying for school; she always thought she would marry a professor. She excelled in art, but her parents looked down on artists as poorly educated and non-academic. When she proposed going to art school, they refused to pay for it.

So after high school, Sook Hee launched her higher education at the University of Alaska. Then, about the same time that I went to Cornell, she moved to California to attend the San Francisco Art Institute. After one semester, Mrs. An asked to borrow money Sook Hee had saved for her education, and so, naturally, she sent it. Quitting school for the time being, she worked first as a waitress and then for Bank of America. Her mother, scared about upcoming thyroid surgery, summoned Sook Hee to return to Anchorage to be near her. So Sook Hee left San Francisco and found a bank job back in Anchorage. That was why she was there when I visited at Christmastime.

As it turned out, she never did finish getting her college degree, although she certainly made an effort. Over the years, she has taken so many classes that she could have earned several degrees. Even without one, she has become a gifted painter in oil, watercolor, and pastel, as well as a fine sculptor. Art is her lifelong avocation.

Sook Hee sums it up this way: "I could have been a success in either art or fashion design or in the banking business, but instead, I followed Steve and raised our children. In essence, I painted on my children's lives. I have no regrets. Unlike some of my successful artist friends, who are all alone, I am not. God had a plan."

POPPING THE QUESTION

One cold and lonely night in Chicago, I placed a phone call to Sook Hee. I had recently sent her a cassette tape on which I had recorded an original love song. Really, it was more like a proposal song:

When this world quickly passes me by, leaving me behind in its memories

I may think that no one cares for me, but when I think of you, you make things all right.

I care for you and I miss you; you've turned my world upside down and I love you.

I know you and I will make it, together we will see tomorrow.

Although we may see some rough waters, I know with our love, we'll make it through.

I cleared my throat several times. Perhaps she thought I was going to sing to her. Then I said, "Sook Hee, I have a question to ask you."

She thought, *Here we go again. I remember what he asked in the Sears Mall....* "What's your question?"

I took a deep breath and popped the question, "Sook Hee, will you marry me?" I was thinking, *What are the odds? Yes or no—that's a 50-50 chance.* (In reality, there was probably a one in a billion chance!)

"Yes, I will marry you."

Huh? She said yes? I regrouped. "I don't think you understood my question. Would you marry me, please?"

"I said, '*Yes,* I will marry you.'"

I was so shocked, I didn't know what do to next. I covered the receiver with my hand and shouted, "Yahoo!" (Which she heard anyway.)

So that was that. Sook Hee and I had never dated at all, and now we were engaged.

The next day, she was still in her pajamas—and puffy-eyed from crying the night before because she had told her mother about my proposal—when the doorbell rang. She answered it to find two strangers standing there in the snow: my high school buddies Richard and Jon, holding out a big bouquet of a dozen red roses. I had asked them to be my delivery men.

Sook Hee gathered up her roses and took them inside, but she did not tell her father what they were for. She knew he'd go ballistic, so she waited to tell him until a week before she was about to leave for Chicago to marry me. Her mother helped her keep the secret. Mr. An did react as she'd expected, but by then, it was too late.

She did not want it to look as if she had just run away, and she did want to obtain some kind of a paternal blessing on her plans. She told her father—referring back to her earlier engagement—that given the choice between a man who was healthy in body, but weak in mind, and a man who was weak in body, but healthy in mind, she wanted to choose the latter.

"There are two kinds of guys," she said. "Some look good on the outside, but their insides are all messed up. Some may be handicapped on the outside, but their insides are good. That's Steve."

Mr. An retaliated with threats, but he had to assent. "Okay, then," he said. "But if you ever get divorced and leave Steve, I won't call you my daughter anymore."

Her uncle found out later, too, and he thought I'd brainwashed or hypnotized her: "You *wiilll* marry me!..." He couldn't figure out why in the world she would say yes. I couldn't figure out why in the world she would want to marry me, either, but I was definitely happy about it!

WEATHERING SOME STORMS

So on another cold and wintry day, March 19, 1982, we got married, having set the date during spring break so that I wouldn't miss any classes. We put on our best outfits and went to the justice of the peace in Skokie, Illinois, with so many of my friends in attendance that the ceremony had to be moved from the judge's chambers to the courtroom. On that day, we experienced rain, sleet, and snow all within a few hours, which was sadly predictive of what our marriage would be like for years to come.

I took all the money I had and splurged on a diamond wedding ring and matching earrings, as well as a Caribbean cruise (inside cabin) for our honeymoon. Now, I realize how shocking it must have been for Sook Hee to see my surgery-scarred body and polio deformities, but she never said anything about it. If the truth be told, both of us had many invisible scars that would become more apparent in the years to come.

Two months after we became Mr. and Mrs. Steve Stirling, I received my master's degree in business management. I had come a long way from the orphanage in Ilsan, earning degrees from two of the top schools in the United States. Out of an array of employment opportunities with Fortune 500 companies—including Pepsi, General Mills, General Foods, Searle (NutraSweet), and Ore-Ida—I decided to stick with Johnson & Johnson's subsidiary, McNeil Consumer Products, where I had interned.

I had graduated at the height of the "stagflation" of 1982, when there was high inflation combined with high interest rates. In such an economic climate, unemployment was high, too, so I was very fortunate to get so many job offers.

We moved from Illinois to Walnut Creek, California, for my sales training. Our life together was launched. How would we handle it?

Sadly, we were not prepared for what was ahead.

Steve as a baby in his father's arms.

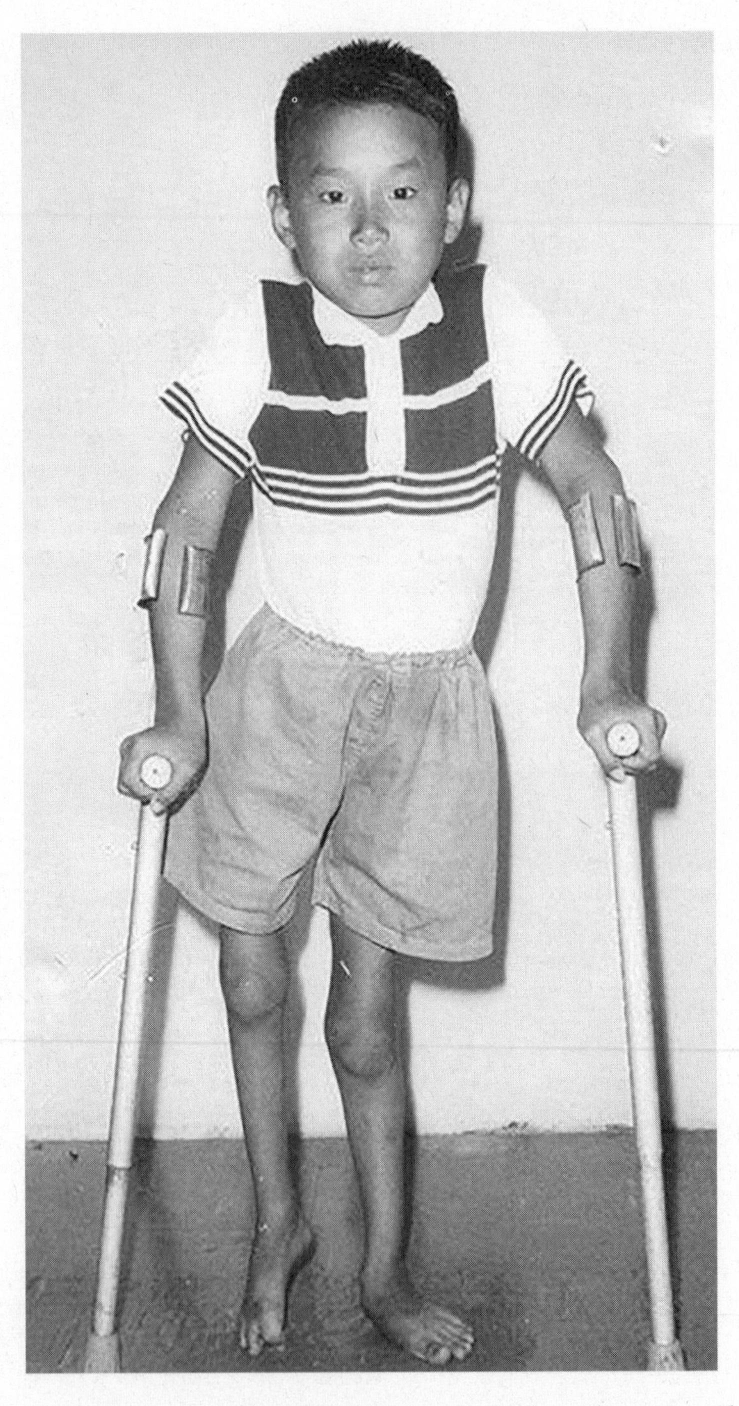

Steve received his first pair of crutches at the Holt orphanage in Ilsan.

89TH CONGRESS
1ST SESSION

H. R. 8219

IN THE HOUSE OF REPRESENTATIVES

MAY 17, 1965

MR. JOHNSON of California introduced the following bill; which was referred to the Committee on the Judiciary

A BILL

For the relief of Cho Myung Soon and Cho Myung Hee.

1 *Be it enacted by the Senate and House of Representa-*
2 *tives of the United States of America in Congress assembled,*
3 That, in the administration of the Immigration and Na-
4 tionality Act, Cho Myung Soon and Cho Myung Hee may
5 be classified as eligible orphans within the meaning of sec-
6 tion 101 (b) (1) (F) of the Act, upon approval of a petition
7 filed in their behalf by Mr. and Mrs. Alexander J. Stirling,
8 citizens of the United States, pursuant to section 205 (b) of
9 the Act, subject to all the conditions in that section relating
10 to eligible orphans.
11 Section 205 (c) of the Immigration and Nationality Act,

III

U.S. House Resolution 8219 enabled Jim and Lyn Stirling to adopt Steve and his sister.

Steve, front row at left, is shown with his family in Alaska.

Steve plays the guitar for friends during his study abroad in France.

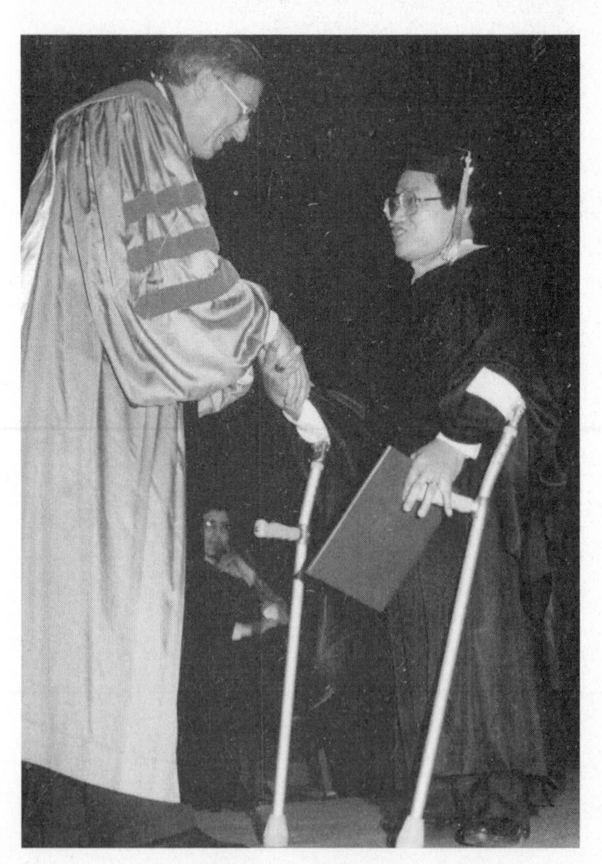

Steve graduated from the Kellogg Graduate School of Management at Northwestern University in June 1982.

Steve and Sook Hee were married by a justice of the peace on March 19, 1982, in Skokie, Illinois.

Steve's mom, Lyn Stirling,
and Sook Hee playfully hug Steve in 1986 in Alaska.

Steve met "Grandma" Bertha Holt in 1988.

Steve reunited with his biological family in 1991.

Emulating his father, Steve took his young son, Richard, fishing in Alaska. Sook Hee's uncle, Charles Nevada, holds the net.

During one of their visits to Korea, Steve and Sook Hee met Myung-Bak Lee, then mayor of Seoul, who served as South Korea's president from 2008 to 2013.

While serving as executive vice president of marketing for Heifer International, Steve's travels took him to Tibet.

Steve joined MAP International in 2014. The blue box he's holding is MAP's Medical Mission Pack, recognized by mission teams and customs officials around the world.

Among other health and medical efforts, MAP has implemented programs to fight neglected tropical diseases. Steve visited Uganda in February 2015. Below, he gives deworming medication to a child in Côte d'Ivoire.

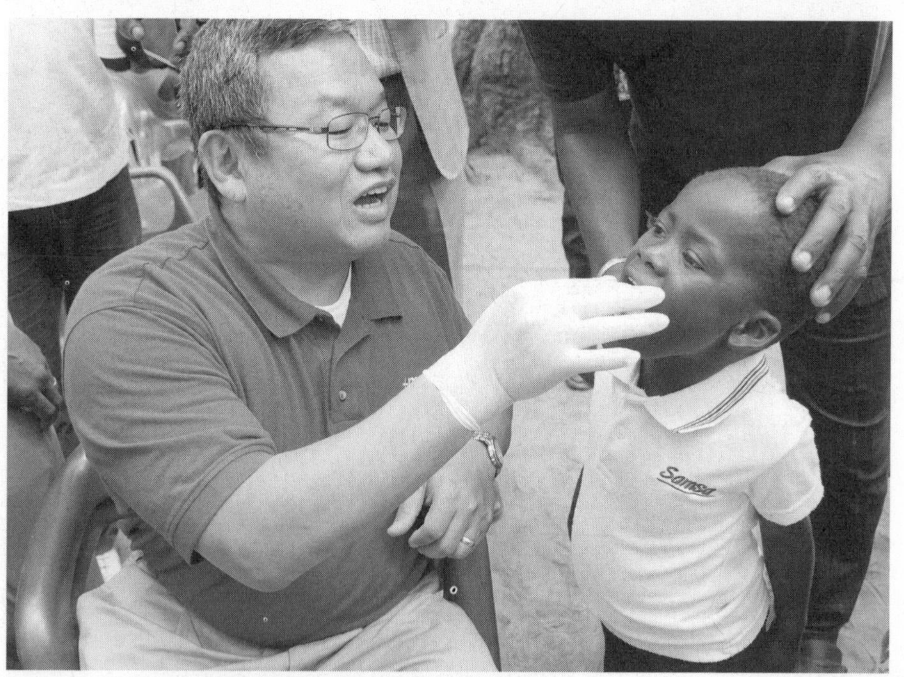

Steve and MAP International Board Chairman Jim Barfoot visit Ecuador in August 2016.

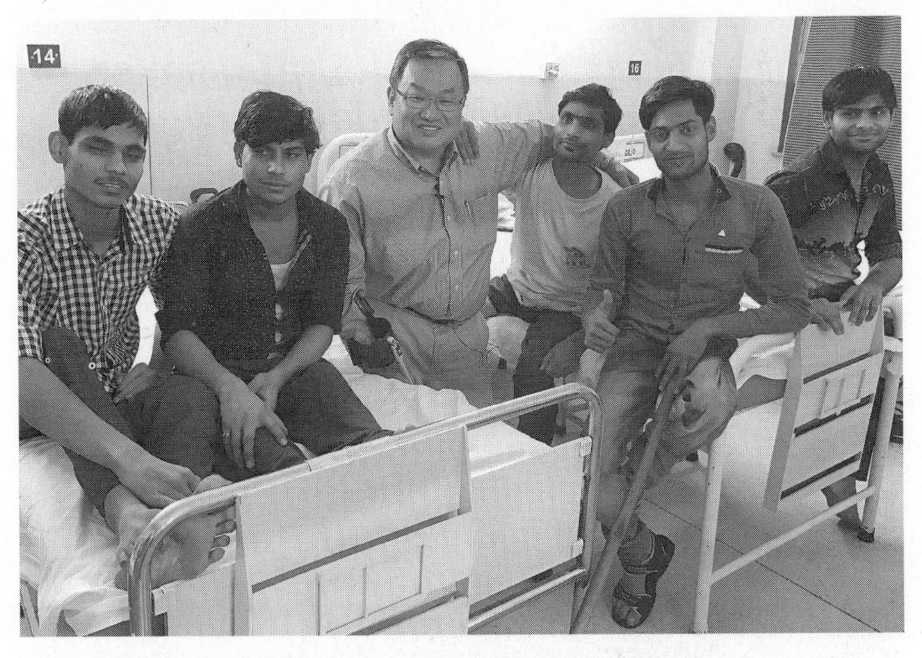

Steve met with polio survivors in India in 2017 during an immunization outreach effort by Rotary International.

Love A Child Founder Bobby Burnette, left, is shown with MAP's former chairman, Phil Mazzilli, center, and Steve Stirling during their visit to Haiti in August 2017.
Below, Love A Child Founder Sherry Burnette greets Steve.

Steve meets with children in Bolivia, top, and Liberia. Everywhere he goes, Steve encourages children to be immunized to protect against disease.

Sook Hee is occasionally able to accompany Steve on his outreach missions for MAP International.

Steve and Sook Hee are shown with their children,
Racheal and Richard.

Bill Foege, left, watches as Steve presents the 2018 Bill Foege Global Health Award to Rosalynn Carter and President Jimmy Carter for their work in eradicating disease and promoting mental health services globally.

Steve meets with Dr. Sanjay Gupta, CNN's chief medical correspondent, during the 2018 Bill Foege Global Health Awards program.

7

ROUGH SAILING

Better one handful with tranquility than two handfuls with toil and chasing after the wind.
—Ecclesiastes 4:6 (NIV)

The first few months were not bad. We liked living in the Bay area. Sook Hee got a job at Bank of America (same bank as before, different branch), to which she commuted daily on the Bay Area Rapid Transit. For the five months of my training starting in June 1982, I was going to be learning on the job by calling on retailers around San Francisco, marketing Tylenol products, after which we would move back east to McNeil headquarters in Fort Washington, Pennsylvania, near Philadelphia.

Tylenol, the brand name for the pain-relieving and fever-reducing drug acetaminophen, had become one of the best-selling over-the-counter pain relievers in the United States.

One Friday evening in late September, after I got home from work, I turned on the TV news and was shocked at what I saw. At the same moment, the phone rang. It was my McNeil district manager. "Steve, a terrible thing has happened in Chicago, and it's all over the news. At least three people have been killed by cyanide-laced Tylenol capsules."

I was stunned. *How could this occur?* I was told to sit tight and wait for instructions. At that point, nobody knew how it had happened, who was at fault, or what to do. Within a short time, four more people had died. Even though it became clear that the deadly capsules had been tampered with after they were on the store shelves, we knew we could not market a product that was potentially lethal. There was a random murderer out there.[10] People were understandably alarmed.

My sales training quickly turned into an excellent education in crisis management. Within a few days, Johnson & Johnson CEO James Burke coolly ordered the nationwide recall of the 31 million Tylenol capsules that had already been distributed, at the expense of $100 million to the company—one of the first major product recalls in history. Sales dropped 80 percent. The brand was expected to tank. The assumption was that nobody in their right mind would want to take another Tylenol capsule, and the best policy seemed to be one of withdrawing into the background until consumers started to forget about what had happened.

But instead of caving in to those expectations, the company was looking into the best ways to create tamper-resistant packaging. This tragedy abruptly forced Johnson & Johnson and the McNeil task forces to devise safer packaging—and all the other manufacturers followed suit. That's when we started to see the triple-sealed packaging with which we have now become so familiar: foil-sealed and shrink-wrapped

10. The Tylenol murderer was never found. To read more about how the Tylenol crisis was handled, see David A. Vise's article "Tylenol: Signs of a Recovery," *The Washington Post*, archived at https://www.washingtonpost.com/archive/business/1982/12/19/tylenol-signs-of-a-recovery/bd16a39c-52ea-489f-a5a2-9438cb283e27/ and Thomas Moore's "The Fight to Save Tylenol," originally published in *Fortune* magazine November 1982 and republished on Oct. 7, 2012, archived at http://fortune.com/2012/10/07/the-fight-to-save-tylenol-fortune-1982.

bottles inside double-glued paperboard boxes. Everyone knew you could never produce a tamper*proof* package because that would be impossible for customers themselves to open. But the term "tamper-resistant" was added to the national vocabulary that year.

Incredibly, by early December, Tylenol was back on the shelves. Of crucial importance was the way the Johnson & Johnson leaders had conducted themselves in an honest and open manner throughout the entire crisis. As the production facilities worked day and night to restock shelves with repackaged Tylenol, people started to purchase it once more. Soon, consumer confidence was restored and we could breathe again. We moved back across the country to Pennsylvania in the middle of the crisis.

This tumultuous year marked the beginning of my corporate experiences with pharmaceutical and health-related products, which I have found invaluable as I moved into my later career with health-related nonprofits.

LAUNCHED IN THE CORPORATE WORLD

I really liked working. I was always excited to get up in the morning, learn new things, and apply what I'd learned in business school. Business school gets your foot in the door, but the real training is when you're actually doing the work. I was working with advertising companies, going to training sessions, applying what I had learned about marketing forecasts, and attending sales meetings. At McNeil and Johnson & Johnson, I had the best of the best to learn from, and I really enjoyed what I was doing. Also, I was making pretty good money.

With Sook Hee working, too, we soon had saved enough to purchase our first home—a townhouse in the Lansdale/North Wales area north of Philadelphia. She began to attend Moore College of Art & Design in the city, and she was thinking about transferring to the

Fashion Institute of Technology (FIT) in New York. On the surface, at least, our life was moving along well.

However, in terms of the corporate lifestyle, I was finding it difficult to break into the culture. (Women often have the same problem.) A lot of business is conducted on golf courses or basketball courts, and I obviously do not play either sport. Those same guys would have parties after work, and those were times to build relationships. I could go down at lunchtime and work out at the gym that was in the building, and I tried to be part of that way of life. But for the most part, I was on the outside looking in, not only because of my physical disability, but also because of my ethnic background.

Still, I could work hard—and I did. (In later years, I used to advise my son, probably too often, "You have to be twice as good as a white person because they're going to look at you differently. The only way to get anyone's attention is to become really successful." I was speaking from my own experience, however, which would not necessarily be his.) I felt strongly that the world is not fair, and I could make it better through productive work and taking a forward-looking approach to everything.

I was still motivated by that strong desire not to let anyone down. First, I'd had my parents in mind, then it was the educators who had given me such wonderful opportunities. I did not want to flop and fail, and somehow prevent other people with disabilities from getting an education at Cornell or Northwestern. I didn't want to disappoint anybody.

But that desire not to let anyone down did not seem to translate into my marriage. I let Sook Hee down all the time. Since she and I had never dated, we had to get to know each "on the job," after the wedding. And we were doing it with as many steep ups and downs as a roller coaster.

At home as well as at work, I couldn't stop trying to prove that I was as good as others, which meant proving I was superior. Marriage should not be a competition, but I treated it that way. Even worse, I could never admit I was wrong. To my way of thinking, acknowledging my mistakes would show weakness or that there was something wrong with me, and others, including my wife, would reject me. What a mistaken assumption! I never could apologize to Sook Hee for anything, whether minor or major, and I certainly could not humble myself enough to ask for forgiveness.

LOOKING FOR MEANING

Sook Hee had to find her personal validation elsewhere, and one of the places was at the Moore College of Art & Design, where she excelled as a student. She seemed to have a special talent for fashion design. On one occasion, she was the only one in the school, including teachers, who managed to figure out the complexities of how something was designed. Everyone was impressed with her abilities.

But our home life was imploding, and she was in distress. My ten-year plan had evolved into a year-by-year plan, which included a plan for each month, each week, and, of course, each hour of each day. I tried to control everything. One day, she said to me, "You know, Steve, I don't want to be a widow. I think you are going to kill yourself with all this planning and all this intensity. If you want to live longer, you're going to have to make a choice. And if you keep up all this planning of yours, and I have to follow it, we're going to have to divorce. I cannot live like this."

Then finally, she couldn't take it anymore. She said, "I'm leaving you. I can't live my life this kind of way. I don't want any money. I just want to say *good-bye*!" She packed her clothes, cut up her credit cards in front of me, and went to stay with one of her classmates. I didn't know what to do to get her back.

I knew she was going to be at a fashion show presented by her school, so I attended it. I saw her and went over to her, but she was looking at someone else. The vice president of OshKosh B'gosh, the children's clothing company, had just come up to her, telling her about an excellent job that she could have when she finished school. When I overheard Sook Hee being complimented for her talents, I realized that she was a gifted woman, valuable and smart. She did not have a college degree, and her broken English embarrassed me, yet she was a top student, an independent individual, not someone who needed to be controlled. I was impressed, and I apologized. Sook Hee believed me when I said I would treat her better at home, and she came back.

Still, our strife continued. I hardly changed at all, and neither of us knew what to do about it.

Throughout this time, Sook Hee sought personal support through her strong Buddhist faith. I had no interest in such things, but to keep her happy, I went with her to temples and listened to her when she told me what she was learning.

ANOTHER JOB OFFER, ANOTHER MOVE

In fact, Sook Hee could never finish at Moore or work for OshKosh because we moved again. Before our third wedding anniversary, I accepted a job offer that would take us to New York City. We sold our townhouse, rented places briefly in Greenwich Village and Soho, and then we moved to Hazlet, New Jersey, where we bought a classic Cape Cod home. I felt that my new position with American Home Products,[11] which involved the launch of the new over-the-counter pain reliever, Advil, was worth the grueling four-hour daily commute by transit. As adept as I was with my crutches, I found that they made it impossible to carry what I needed for my long days, such as a businessman's raincoat

11. American Home Products (Whitehall Labs) was later renamed Wyeth and is now part of Pfizer.

or umbrella. My briefcase was all I could manage, and the cheap plastic rain poncho I carried for bad weather made me look like a street person. Meanwhile, Sook Hee worked for MasterCard and was quickly promoted.

We were only seven months into our new routine when everything screeched to a halt. I needed an emergency appendectomy. I'd had a lot of experience with polio surgery, but nothing compared to this. What would have been a straightforward operation for anyone else was greatly complicated by the way my internal organs are packed into my polio-twisted torso. Instead of entailing only a little incision, the appendectomy required major abdominal surgery. I had to stay in the hospital for a week.

While I was at home convalescing, I got a call from one of my best friends, Carl Wright, about a senior product manager position that was opening up at Mead Johnson Nutritionals in Evansville, Indiana. At first, I said, "No, thanks. I can't change jobs again right now. I just did." But then when I considered the rigors of commuting four or five hours a day to New York City versus driving twenty minutes in a car, it sounded enticing. I took the opportunity. Once again, Sook Hee quit her job and began to pack for a move.

We drove to Evansville, arriving ahead of the moving van. We were in a temporary living situation, and I was nursing a cold when the phone rang. "Mr. Stirling, I have some bad news. The moving truck caught fire, and all of your furniture and possessions are gone."

Is this for real? What next? Everything we owned either had been incinerated or had sustained irreparable smoke damage. *Well, okay…nothing is meant to last forever, right?* Rallying fast, we negotiated with a local furniture company to furnish our new home, and they delivered the bed immediately so at least we'd have a place to sleep over the weekend while we waited for the rest of the furniture to be delivered. Problem solved, right?

Not so fast. Over the weekend, like a bad dream, the furniture store went up in flames! Whoever heard of such a sequence of events?

FROM ROLLER COASTER TO ROCK-A-BYE BABY

Married only three years, we had already moved half a dozen times. It seemed as though we had lost and regained ground too many times already, in every part of our lives: marriage, finances, and possessions. We had been through some mighty rough sailing and needed to find something to anchor us in the midst of the turbulence.

At Mead Johnson Nutritionals, part of the Bristol-Myers Squibb Company, I expanded my marketing expertise from consumer pharmaceuticals to health-promoting nutrition products, such as infant formulas and baby foods. I was going to be involved in the American launch of Milupia, a baby food from Germany.

Infant formula? Baby food? Hey, maybe having a child of our own would stabilize things a little. But having a baby wouldn't necessarily be any easier than anything else had been. We would probably encounter fertility problems related to my polio. In addition, historically, all of the women in Sook Hee's family had found it difficult to conceive.

She wanted to pray about it. To whom should she pray, though? Buddhists do not pray to a supreme Creator as Christians do. Her forays into spiritual things and philosophy had not given her an answer to that question. One night, she heard an internal voice saying, "Pray to the One who can create life." She also had two visions. In the first, she was holding onto a big rope that was coming apart. In the second, she saw two towers at a temple in Gyeongju, Korea, which is important to Buddhism, with a big rock coming toward Sukka tower, knocking it down and scattering it to pieces. She didn't know anything yet about Jesus being called the Rock.

Most of her childhood experiences with Christianity had been bad ones. If the name of Jesus or anything Christian-sounding had been mentioned, she would have turned away from it. All her life, she had studied Eastern and Western philosophies, especially Buddhism and Confucianism, and they had a lot of influence on her thinking. (In addition, she had not really wanted children until we moved to Indiana, having grown up with so much instability in her family life. She used to assume she would marry a man with many children already.)

For seven days, she prayed to Whoever Can Create, asking for a child. A week later, as she was praying during the night, lying on her side, a bright cross-shaped light flashed on the bedroom wall. Simultaneously, she had an inner sense about three things: she would become pregnant; she would give birth to a son; and she and I needed to go to church.

Two weeks later, she discovered she was pregnant. She shared the good news with me, of course, but she was afraid to tell me about her nighttime experiences. She did insist that we go to church.

"Oh, who's getting married?" I asked. I really didn't get it. Then she told me about her visions and other spiritual experiences, but we didn't go to church right away.

In November 1986, our son Richard was born. Just as the Stirlings had named me Steven Glenn after my father's best friends, so I named our son Richard after my best friend Richard, with whom I had shared so many good times.

After Richard was born, I did agree to attend church with my wife. We decided to attend the Baptist church that was close by, on our street. It seemed appropriate to attend our first service on Mother's Day

1987. We were so thankful for Richard, our healthy baby boy. Since we weren't really Christians yet, we had no context for the pastor's sermon, which centered on a line from the Bible: "*When my father and my mother forsake me, then the Lord will take me up*" (Psalm 27:10 KJV). What kind of thing was that to say on Mother's Day? What was the pastor talking about?

We went home, willing to give the church another chance the next week. Guess what the pastor preached on the next week? Tithing. We just happened to hit that particular Sunday. Now, he was asking for 10 percent of our money. I just sat there thinking, *They don't even know us and they want our money. What is this about?* They also sent us a letter about tithing. We found this a little upsetting.

I mentioned it to a Christian friend who had been my neighbor growing up in Alaska and had also moved to Evansville, so he invited us to visit his church, Christian Fellowship Church. The church sponsors Bible study fellowship groups, and we started to attend services and classes. CFC was a very large church with over three thousand members.

After a little while, Pastor David Niednagel asked who wanted to be baptized. We put our names on the sign-up sheet, but we didn't really know what we were agreeing to. After we failed to show up for the pre-baptism class, he took the time to visit us in our home to explain to us what baptism means—and also what the gospel message is. He shared a few passages from Scripture with us:

> "*For all have sinned and fall short of the glory of God*"
> (Romans 3:23)

> "*For the wages of sin is death, but the gift of God is eternal life in Christ Jesus our Lord*" (Romans 6:23)

> *"For God so loved the world that He gave His only begotten Son, that whoever believes in Him should not perish but have everlasting life"* (John 3:16)

> *"For by grace you have been saved through faith, and that not of yourselves; it is the gift of God, not of works, lest anyone should boast"* (Ephesians 2:8–9)

When Pastor Niednagel said, "Jesus loves you more than anybody in the whole world loves you," Sook Hee's heart broke. In all of her spiritual searching, she had never known before that God loved her.

Later, she explained it to me this way: "Jesus loved me so much He died for me?! I had not found anything like that in Buddhism or anywhere else. *They* didn't love me. Reincarnation didn't appeal to me. Love did. I used to think Jesus was like all the others—that you had to earn your way into His presence. And here was this pastor telling me that I didn't have to earn Jesus's love at all. I didn't have to do anything except say 'yes' to Him. I didn't care if I went to heaven or hell, but I *did* care if somebody loved me. The pastor was telling me that Jesus accepts me just as I am. All my life, I had to please other people. I had to be a good daughter, a good wife, a good member of the community, and now a good mother. Wow! Jesus didn't tell me to be good so that He would accept me. I had a lot of evil thoughts, but He loved me anyway. He loved me even if I didn't do anything special for Him. Now I could have a connection with God anytime. I began to cry—and I kept on crying for about three months whenever I was by myself doing chores."

Sook Hee accepted Jesus as her Lord and Savior. Not me, though. I wanted to go to heaven, so I said the right words. But for me, getting baptized felt sort of like buying an insurance policy. It took seven more years before I understood what it meant to accept Jesus as my *Lord* as well as my Savior. I was still holding back from a full surrender of my life. After all, asking Jesus Christ to become the Lord of my life was not part of my ten-year plan, and I did not want anyone telling me what to do.

Both Sook Hee and I got baptized on Father's Day 1987. We could have been baptized in a lake, but they did it by sprinkling because it would have been so difficult for me to take off my leg braces to get into the water. Also, my pride prevented me from allowing someone to carry me into the lake.

Sook Hee wept when she got baptized. This bothered me. "What are you crying about, here in front of people?" *Women are so emotional,* I thought. Then she cried at the drop of a hat for weeks. Something significant had happened in her heart...but not in mine. I dug in my heels. "I don't want to go to church with you. On Sundays, I want to sleep in like we did before. I want to read the Sunday paper."

Our home became a battlefield every Sunday. Sook Hee would get herself and the baby ready for church while I slumbered away in the bed. Still, now she knew who to pray to, and she knew that God heard her prayers. As she struggled to do the right thing, she heard His still small voice again: "Leave Steve to me." And she put me into His hands.

That did not guarantee smooth sailing. Our difficulties only increased as she endeavored to learn how to live her new life in Christ while I carried on a split existence.

SAME SONG, SECOND VERSE

Later that year, I was promoted to director of marketing for another division of Bristol-Myers Squibb. This division was called the Jobst Institute, and they sold healthcare equipment such as compression stockings. Of course, the job change involved another move, this time to Toledo, Ohio. By the time we made that move, Sook Hee was pregnant again. As usual, she had to cope with all of the new challenges single-handedly, since I was so preoccupied with my work, and both of our families were living in Alaska.

She found another church and new friends, both Korean and American, but I was too busy to meet more than a few of them. We settled into our roles as parents, with me as the corporate executive breadwinner and Sook Hee as a stay-at-home mom.

In June, Racheal was born. "Racheal" is a variant of the name Rachelle, which I had first heard and loved when I was in France; it was also the name of one of Sook Hee's best friends. In addition, Sook Hee had read the Bible story about Rachel, who was loved by Jacob, and she wanted our daughter to be loved by her future husband and by God. We were thrilled with our beautiful baby daughter.

Two years prior, when Richard was born by C-section, we had considered tubal ligation, figuring the best thing would be to adopt if we wanted more children. But our Christian pediatrician in Evansville had persuaded us not to have it done. Now, with baby Racheal, we were so grateful. What a treasure we would have missed if we had followed our original plan!

A REUNION OF HOLT ADOPTEES

Toledo is not far from Grand Rapids, Michigan, which is where the Holt adoptees' annual reunion was going to be held just a month after Racheal was born. We decided to attend, especially since Bertha ("Grandma") Holt was going to be there. I had seen her when I was a boy in the orphanage, but not since then. Grandma Holt was then in her eighties, but she was still very active. In fact, people called her "the jogging grandma" because she ran a mile every day. (Even eight years after we talked to her at the picnic, she set the world record for her age group in a four-hundred-meter race.) She also kept busy traveling the world for the Holt adoption programs. In Korea, she had become a kind of Mother Teresa figure, especially after her husband passed away.

At the picnic, she was dressed in a full-length, pale pink *hanbok,* a traditional Korean dress, smiling and holding up her hands in delight. She always wore Korean dresses for special events. Her pure white hair reflected the sunshine. We chatted and took pictures; I was pleased to show her my beautiful family and tell her some things about my life in America.

Seeing her helped to bring things full circle for me. (Grandma Holt's sister Beulah had also played a prominent part in my early life, and we were later able to visit her in Washington State.) Also, having a son and a daughter of my own was starting to make me think about what a difficult and courageous thing it must have been for my father in Korea to have dropped me off at the door of the Holt orphanage. How could a man surrender both his first-born son and then a daughter to strangers? How desperate must he have been—and how grateful I was now for what he had done. His heartbreaking decision had been the right one.

My life was becoming a success story in so many ways...but not where my marriage was concerned. I had so much more to learn. I was working as the director of marketing, with all of the responsibilities that entailed, and I never stopped being critical of Sook Hee at home. I now found fault even more with her achievements, her housekeeping, and her other qualities.

She was not a passive recipient of my mistreatment. We were sullen and angry with each other most of the time. My wife loved being a mother, but she was stretched to the limit. Nevertheless, I was sure we were going to stick it out now, for the children's sake...or would we?

8

SHOOTS AND ROOTS

Rejoice with me, for I have found my sheep which was lost!
—Luke 15:6

Sook Hee kept asking me if I wanted to go back to Korea to search for my biological family. I had no interest in that; I always told her my real parents and siblings were in Alaska. Eventually though, because of my love for my own small son and daughter, I reconsidered. It might not be easy, but we could try. I didn't know if my father was alive or dead, but I wanted to find him and reassure him that his agonizing decision so many years before had been the right one.

Sook Hee had Korean friends at our American church in Toledo, who introduced us to a Korean man with connections to the Korean Central Intelligence Agency or KCIA. As it happened, the KCIA had had generated long lists of names in a people-finding effort that was meant to help reunite families that had been split by the north-south partition. I did not even know the names of my parents, having been abandoned at such a young age. With the KCIA's help, we might be able to get somewhere. We decided to undertake the search.

As a family, we made the more-than-24-hour flight from Detroit via Tokyo to Seoul in April 1991. It must have been a taxing trip for Sook Hee, with two children under four years old and a disabled husband. We were able to stay with her brother, Douglas, who was then married and living in Seoul.

We went first to the Holt orphanage in Ilsan to see if they could furnish any clues. Yes, they could! One name—a fairly distinct one—turned up in their records. Unlike the way I was abandoned, the person who had dropped off Mary Ellen at the orphanage in 1962 had actually signed for her. This person was not a relative, but his very unusual name would make him much easier to look up. Our contact in the KCIA checked the lists and found only two people with that name in the Seoul area. We were given one address, so we went there, but found no one home. Leaving a note about our quest, we gave Douglas's phone number as a means of contacting us.

Within a short time, we got a phone call from my aunt, the one who, as it turned out, had persuaded my father to abandon me! This was an amazing discovery.

The man with the uncommon name was related to her by marriage on her in-laws' side, and he had called her after finding our note. In 1962, she had asked him to serve as the go-between, taking Mary Ellen to Holt so no one would be able to trace her family.

Although my aunt had come from northern Korea as my father had, she could not have taken me into her family when my father was unable to care of me. As a woman in Korean society in those days, she did not have much influence, except to offer advice. In other words, she is not to be blamed for advising our father to abandon us. In an interesting twist to this story, my aunt told us that her son, my cousin, who is a little older than I am, owned a Christian publishing company in Seoul.

NEW NAME, NEW LIFE

While we made contact with my aunt fairly quickly, the family trail turned out to be much more complicated than we imagined. Remember our Korean names, Cho Myung Soo (mine) and Cho Myung Hee (Mary Ellen's)? Evidently, "Cho" had become our family surname only a short time before we were born, after my father was forced to come to South Korea because of the perils of remaining in the north. When he fled—quite possibly leaving a young wife behind—his surname had been Lee. He had been well-educated in Japan and his family was well-to-do, both politically and socially high-ranking; the Lees were descended from a royal lineage. The Lee family is extensive, comprising a number of clans that derive from the Joseon (Chosun) dynasty that lasted five centuries. My family descends from the Jeonju clan, a branch that can trace its origins to the royal family, with its many contributions to modern Korean society. (One 15th century king, Sejong the Great, created the Korean alphabet.) In northern Korea before the war, my family was wealthy, owning orchards and a mine. My grandfather, educated in Japan, was the head of the postal system. But when the communists came, they were executing people like him. Realizing he was in danger, he and his son, my father, escaped to the south just before the war started on June 25, 1950, giving their valuables to the guide who took them out of the country.

After my father fled, to minimize the chances that he could be traced, he decided to take the surname Cho—the last name of a branch of his family by marriage. Moreover, he adopted the identity of a twin baby boy in the Cho family who had died, but whose death had not been reported. Thus he wiped the slate clean and started his life in South Korea as a different person.

At the time, the Korean government was a mess, and the country was impoverished. Korea had achieved independence from Japan and it was no longer a colony, but there were many factions and parties fighting with each other, with the Chinese and Russian involvement making things even more complicated. At first, our father worked as a policeman and then in an office in the capitol building in Seoul.

Mrs. An told Sook Hee about those times. Her experiences would have been different from my family's, but I have to agree with her theory that the reason so many Koreans of that era behave aggressively is because they had to in order to survive. First, Korea was under Japanese occupation, then the country was divided in two after World War II, and then came the Korean War and its unsettled aftermath, with famine and distress everywhere. Even Mrs. An's family, who lived in a farming region and therefore had something to eat, became hungry and malnourished. Life was hard all around.[12]

We will never know very much about that time in my father's life. By the time he had married my mother and started to have children, he was working for the new South Korean government in a communications and security capacity. His new wife, my mother, had not come from the north of Korea as he had.

A JOYOUS AND TEARFUL FAMILY REUNION

Sook Hee spoke with my aunt on the phone, and it was decided that we would all meet up at a particular hotel. (With my insufficient Korean not being up to the task of communicating with my family members, Sook Hee had to do all of the talking and translating. She lost her voice completely by the end of our exhausting visit.)

When we approached the front entrance of the hotel, I saw two women standing there. Without a doubt, we belonged to the same family! One of them looked a lot like Mary Ellen, and the other resembled me. Sure enough, they were my two older sisters.

12. In 1955, South Korea's gross domestic product (GDP) was at the same level as Haiti's.

"How did you know who we were?" they asked Sook Hee after discovering that she could speak Korean, but I couldn't.

"Because," Sook Hee said, nodding at one of them, "you look so much like Steve, and you," nodding toward the other one, "look just like Myung Hee."

They were completely astonished to discover that both of us had been adopted into the same family in America.

My sisters took us inside to meet our mother, a younger brother, an aunt, and as many other family members as could be squeezed into one hotel room. It was emotional, overwhelming, and chaotic.

Sook Hee was barraged with questions. My birth mother and sisters cried and cried. In the midst of it, I was smiling but stunned, reserved. That changed when I beckoned to my brother, who had been standing still in the corner, gesturing to him to come over to me. I embraced him and he hugged me back, weeping. I lost it then, sobbing tears of joy.

None of us had ever expected to see each other again. When the rest of them found out that both of their lost siblings had been adopted into the same American family, they found it almost unbelievable. As soon as we could break away, we phoned Mary Ellen, who was living and working in California, to arrange for her to fly over immediately to meet everyone as well.

We gathered for a few hours at the hotel, then returned to Douglas's house in Seoul, where we had left our children. After Mary Ellen arrived a week later, we went together to my sister's condo, which was in a tall building with many flights of stairs and no elevator. Consequently, once I clambered up all of those stairs, I simply stayed there for several days and nights, sleeping on the floor. Richard and Racheal met their young cousins for the first time. We talked and talked. They shared old photographs with us and gave us some to keep.

Mary Ellen's arrival restarted the whole thing over again, with tears, exclamations, and explanations, all carried on through Sook Hee's non-stop translation. Because Mary Ellen had been so young when she was taken to the orphanage, she didn't remember any of these people, although I remembered some of them. She remembered the orphanage, but she didn't remember living at home with our family. Our older sisters remembered us both, of course. Because they had been told that Mary Ellen had been adopted within Korea, they had searched for her there fruitlessly. Our oldest sister remembers going to sleep at night holding Mary Ellen's hand when she was little.

Mary Ellen felt completely out of her element with all of these people who had suddenly surfaced as her brother, sisters, mother, aunt, and uncle. The whole time, our mother and aunt could not stop patting us on the shoulders, legs, hands, and heads, making tender cries. Thirty years is a long time to be apart.

As grateful as Mary Ellen and I were to have found our long-lost family, we found that we were more grateful to have grown up in what we consider our "real" family, the Stirlings. It was a good thing to find our own people and discover some things about our roots, but we would never want to go back and live it over again.

THE MISSING YEARS

In our endless conversations, we learned a great deal about our history. We had to put it all together later with the additional help of some historical research undertaken by Sook Hee.

As I mentioned, our father had fled the north of Korea when the rumblings of war began. It was prudent to leave before the border between the north and south was closed altogether. We undoubtedly still have numerous relatives in North Korea today. After my father changed his name, he found a position with the wartime government in South Korea under President Syngman Rhee.

At some point, my parents met, married, and started a family. When their first two children turned out to be girls (my two older sisters), they wanted a son so badly that they resorted to a traditional Korean folk belief to ensure that their next child would be a much-desired son—they dressed one of the girls as a boy. We have at least one photograph from this time. Sure enough, the next baby was, in fact, a boy—me! But before I was old enough to walk, I contracted polio and my legs were paralyzed. My parents went on to have another daughter (Mary Ellen) and a son—five children altogether.

My father's work with the South Korean government seems to have involved a combination of roles: Japanese/Korean translator, because he was fluent in Japanese; press secretary/journalist; host and escort for visiting officials from foreign countries; and probably other positions as well. But when the regime changed in 1960—a couple of years before he took me to the orphanage—his employment changed, too. The new short-term government was unstable, and everyone was replaced. My father may have worked as a book translator (Japanese to Korean) during that time. By the time the government of Park Chung-Hee took over in a coup, he re-entered government service.

We can tell from photos of that time that the family home was very nice when he was working for the government and not as nice when he lost his job. However, my parents still had a camera and money to develop the film, so they must not have been too terribly poor.

In the meantime, there was this problem of having a growing son at home who could not walk and would soon be of school age. No kind of care or therapy for polio victims was available in Korea. Our father was good to us, and he did not let his personal problems interfere with love for his children. Without exception, we children loved him back. Not many Korean men would allow a picture to be taken of themselves holding their baby son, but he did. That photograph of him holding me provides concrete evidence of his love.

Around the time of our father's job loss, family difficulties arose. My father did not see eye-to-eye with my mother, which caused problems in their marriage. Our mother remained in our home with our two older sisters and my brother (still a nursing baby), while our father took me and Mary Ellen to stay at his sister's house. When his sister advised him to abandon me to an American-run orphanage in the hopes that I might be taken to the United States, he decided that this might well provide for me better than anything he could ever do, whether or not he was employed. It was during this time that we were brought to Holt. When our mother came back to pick us up at her sister-in-law's house, we weren't there. Of course, she asked where we were and was told, "I don't have them."

"What do you mean, you don't have them?!" She was frantic. This was when they told her that Myung Hee had been adopted by a Korean family, and I had been sent to a family in America. No matter what, our father would not tell her where he had taken us because he was afraid she would go and fetch us.

The family fell apart. Our mother left for good, taking her two remaining daughters. But after a while, when she could no longer support them, she had to put them into an orphanage, too, until she could get back on her feet. This sort of thing happened a lot in those post-war years and orphanages proliferated. Our younger brother stayed with our father. Growing up, he claims he never saw our father smile. We think that giving away his son and his daughter must have had something to do with that.

In due course, both of our parents remarried, and neither one of them told their new spouses that they had other, "lost" children. Eventually, someone told our father's new wife, but our mother never did tell her husband. Although our father had died by the time we visited, we met our stepmother and found her to be a gentle, kind person, a Christian believer who had prayed for us without ever having known us. Together, our father and stepmother had two more sons, our half-brothers, with whom we keep in touch.

When we visited in 1991, my brother told me that since my name was still in the paperwork, I had legal rights to inherit family assets as the oldest son. I reassured him that I didn't want my share. We also found out that our mother was a lifelong Catholic and she told me she had prayed daily for my sister and me for all the years she was separated from us. After returning to the U.S., both Mary Ellen and I talked with her on the phone often.

SOOK HEE MAKES A DISCOVERY

Toward the end of that first visit, we all went together back to Ilsan to see where Mary Ellen and I had lived for four years. The sight of so many disabled people made Sook Hee realize why disabled people did not bother her. She remembered she'd had quite a few disabled school friends prior to meeting me, and more than once, she had visited orphanages to play with kids from school when she still lived in Korea. Because she was so accustomed to being with disabled people and orphans, she felt altogether comfortable with me. She simply saw everyone as a person, whether orphaned or disabled or not. She'd also had a friend in Anchorage who'd had polio. As she was growing up, God had been preparing her to marry me.

After three weeks in Korea, we had to go home again. We have kept in touch with my family members and have been able to see each other again five or six times over the years. In fact, we were able to get my mother a plane ticket to come to the U.S. when Mary Ellen got married. She was also able to visit us in Evansville and become acquainted with her grandchildren, Richard and Racheal, as well as Mary Ellen's daughter, Jasmine. When my mother met our adoptive mom, she thanked her profusely, telling her, "Thank you, Lyn, for taking care of my children, for giving them life and love."

My Korean mother lived to a ripe old age, passing away in 2016, at peace with the way everything had turned out. Sook Hee traveled to Korea to be with her before she died, although work obligations kept me at home.

I wish my father could have lived to see me and Mary Ellen, grown and thriving.

9

PAST, PRESENT, FUTURE

For we are His workmanship,
created in Christ Jesus for good works,
which God prepared beforehand that we should walk in them.
—Ephesians 2:10

Back in Evansville, I plunged back into the rat race. Bristol-Meyers Squibb had sold the Jobst division to a German company, Beiersdorf A.G., makers of Nivea. I now worked as director of the adult nutritional division of Mead Johnson Nutritionals (MJN). Not for long, however. Downsizing meant demotion for me; I became senior product manager for the nutritional drink, Nutrament.

As part of their reorganization, MJN had a rule that you had to have at least six people reporting to you, or you couldn't be a vice president or a director. I did have six people reporting to me, but my general manager had only two people reporting to him: the head of marketing (me) and the head of sales. So to help make up his six, he took away four of my people, thus demoting me! It wasn't a bad development, really, because I did not have to take a cut in pay, yet I had much less responsibility.

As far as my family was concerned, this demotion was certainly a good thing because it meant I could have more quality time with them. I could also reflect a little more about my life, as God moved me into position for the next stage of His plan for me.

God had been coaching Sook Hee about a new approach to being my wife. He had told her something like this: "You will be the shadow, behind Steve. I will use Steve for my glory. He will be in front of you." She decided to take it on faith that I would be out in front of her in spiritual matters and she would support my efforts, even though the evidence seemed to contradict that. She recorded for future reference: "I may have more knowledge of the Bible and all that, but Steve will be out in front. It reminds me of Moses, how he said, 'I am not the articulate talker.' I am not as articulate as he is, and I choose to believe that God will use his abilities for His glory and His sake."

It would prove to be prophetic, but it wasn't going to happen overnight. Some further humbling had to happen first.

A SCHEDULE FOR EVERYTHING

After all the twists and turns my career had taken, I was getting a little more realistic about hanging on to any kind of a ten-year plan, but I was still trying to be in complete control at home. Sook Hee can testify that I was an impossible stickler for scheduling my months, my weeks, my days, my hours—and hers. Vacations were the worst. I would set a pace that would obliterate any sense of relaxation for the family, a punishing sequence of events and activities. Up bright and early, I would push us to keep with the daily regimen and would express great irritation if we slipped behind. "We're supposed to be finished with this already and we're overdue at the next activity!" Nobody got a break.

Exasperated, Sook Hee heard that Promise Keepers, the Christian men's organization, was going to hold a stadium event in nearby

Indianapolis. Without consulting me, she signed me up to go with the men from the Evansville Christian Fellowship Church. I really did not want to do it, but I agreed, feeling manipulated.

Right up until the day of the event, I increased the pressure on Sook Hee. I was holding the reins in every category except the one that mattered most: loving spiritual leadership. She chronicled what happened: "Steve is giving me such a hard time. But when I read the Bible, I see that the man had to be the head of the family, spiritually leading and guiding. When I go to church, I see all the husbands and fathers and they are living that way—or so I think. I remember that God had told me to be Steve's shadow. But he is doing the opposite of leading me spiritually. What should I do?"

She was under so much pressure that she reacted with violent anger when Richard did something wrong. She spanked him much too hard and sent him to bed. Racheal was already in bed and so was I.

Afterward, she said, "I felt so bad. I knew I had taken out my anger at my husband on my eight-year-old child. I was angry at God, too. I said to Him, 'You say that the husband is supposed to be the godly head of the family. But Steve is totally not the head of this family. Do you still want me married to this guy?'

"I was still a baby Christian, and I had been studying Moses and the Law and the prophets—very heavy stuff. I was weighed down with legalism and oppression. I couldn't take it anymore. I decided to leave right then and there.

"I took off in the car, leaving my sleeping family in the house. It was nighttime and it started to pour down rain. I couldn't see to drive, so I pulled over. I had my fist up to God. I told Him, 'I don't want this kind of life! I'm a bad mother. I'm turning into an abusive mother!" I burst into tears, fighting with God. Then—sometimes God can be really humorous—an inner voice said, 'Okay, you can run away from them. But if you do, go home first and tell your kids that you are running away because of your husband, not because of them.' I thought of Richard, crying himself to sleep because of the spanking I'd given him. That's the last thing he knew and I didn't want him to think that my leaving was his fault. So I decided to go back and tell the kids I was running away, not because of them but because of their dad.

"I went back home and woke Steve up. 'Hey, did you know I just ran away?' He was grouchy and sarcastic. So I decided to tell the kids the very next day, at the end of the day when we would all be together for dinner. Then I would announce that we were going to split. I didn't tell Steve, and he didn't suspect what I was thinking.

"The next day after the kids went to school and Steve went to work, I called some of my friends, who were very strong women of faith, and said, 'Pray for me!' Then I lay down in front of the Lord, both physically and spiritually. I had been telling Steve what he should do for too long: 'Come to church. Study the Bible. Go to Promise Keepers.' I surrendered. 'Lord, I give up. Steve is my husband. He is not my kid. If you want to change him, change him. I'm going to leave everything to you.'

"God spoke to me in response, saying, 'Sook Hee, I will take care of Steve. But you must change, also.' Then He gave me the Bible verse I had been studying already, the one about removing the log in your own eye."

Sook Hee decided to stay and she never made her evening announcement to the family. The next week, I went off to Promise Keepers, never suspecting that so many prayers were about to be answered.

UNDERSTANDING THE SIN OF PRIDE

The Indianapolis Hoosier Dome was packed to capacity with over 62,000 men, young and old; they said it was the biggest Promise Keepers event to date. We listened to a series of speakers, cheering and clapping as if we were at a football game, especially when legendary coach Bill McCartney, the founding director of Promise Keepers, spoke. Men were doing the wave, chanting, "We love Jesus, yes we do! We love Jesus! How 'bout you?"

How about me? Could I say that I loved Jesus?

Not really.

I had always thought of myself as a Christian and I had acknowledged Jesus as my Savior, but in practice, I had remained my own master and lord. My underlying belief was that you had to earn your way into God's graces just as you had to earn good grades in school. I worked hard to please my superiors and—at least to my way of thinking—to be a good person, as my parents had taught me to be. I knew I was not perfect, but I didn't think of myself as a sinner.

It all came together when the evening speaker said, "The worst sin is pride because it steals God's glory."

The story of my life flashed before me in vivid focus. I realized that God had answered every one of my prayers. Every single one! *God* had been the one who had done everything, not me! He deserved all of the credit, and yet I'd taken it myself. He had picked me up when I was an abandoned kid in Korea, and He had placed me in a loving family. He had gotten me into the best universities. He had given me a beautiful wife and children. I was living the American dream because of His loving care. And what was I doing? Taking all the credit and glory.

I was stealing God's glory. I was proud and self-sufficient. I could never admit when I was wrong. I had never really humbled myself before Him.

I had made Jesus my Savior when I got baptized because I want to go to heaven when I die. But—a huge "but"—I had not made Him my *Lord*. I was rarely allowing God to direct my life. I was not following Him as a disciple. I still had my ten-year plan to follow. I was not allowing God to guide me, correct me, or strengthen me. I was talking to Him, usually to ask Him for something, but I was not listening to His still, small voice. (See 1 Kings 19:12.)

For my whole life, the Lord Jesus had been beckoning me, and I had not really heard Him. I had prayed to God and He had answered me. How could I have been so blind? I had appreciated His many gifts, but I had taken all the credit. I had stolen His glory.

I humbled myself and did the only thing left to do: I asked God to forgive me for stealing His glory. I told Him I wanted Him to be my *Lord* as well as my Savior.

I cannot overemphasize the importance of making Jesus both Savior and Lord. Accepting Him as Savior cleanses you from guilt and sin; you accept His forgiveness, your sins are atoned for through His death and resurrection, and you are headed to heaven. But that is only the beginning of the story. It is not the same as new life in Christ, which begins only when you accept Him as Lord. When you make Jesus your Lord, you begin to take your marching orders from Him, and you become a real disciple. From then on, you no longer call the shots—He does. This is a total reorientation, and it affects every part of your daily life. You place yourself in God's hands, which is the best place to be.

A NEW AND BETTER BEGINNING

Later that summer, Sook Hee signed me up to be a leader for our weekend church camp. I was assigned to a cabin full of hyperactive boys, ten to twelve years old, and I brought my guitar to help calm things down in the evening. I played a little and then I told a Bible story.

Everyone was quietly listening when a boy named Brandon spoke up. "Mr. Stirling, I want to accept Jesus as my Savior and Lord."

I was startled. What should I do? "Brandon, you don't have to do that until you're ready."

He said, "Well, I heard the story and I'm ready to accept Jesus as my Savior and Lord."

"Are you sure? Do you know what that means?" (What was I doing, trying to turn him away?)

He persisted, "Yes, I know I'm a sinner and I want to accept Jesus."

"Uh, okay." I led him in the prayer of salvation.

The wording of the prayer varies depending on circumstances. We prayed something like this:

> "Dear Lord, I know I am not perfect, and I do many selfish things that do not measure up to Your holiness. I am truly sorry and I ask You to forgive me. I believe that You died on the cross to save me from my sins and that You love me. I give my life to You, and I ask You to help me live for You from this day forward. I want You to be my Savior and my Lord. Thank You and amen."

Brandon recited this prayer and he meant every word of it.

It broke me to think that God had used me to lead someone to Christ. On my bottom bunk that night while the boys slept, I shed silent tears. "Lord, why would You use me? I didn't want to come here, and I even tried to turn this boy away, yet You used me to bring him to Yourself."

Brandon was the first of many people I led to Christ. I used to keep a running list, and I tried to pray for them all by name, but after a few years, the list got too long. I reached out to anyone who would listen, and I started to pray for "divine appointments" when I went to an airport, the gym, or even the sauna.

What had happened at Promise Keepers had a far-reaching effect on my life. Until I accepted Jesus as my Lord, I had always felt a kind of emptiness. I was always seeking something, always trying to achieve more and more, to prove that I was acceptable. After Promise Keepers, I found purpose. I could even begin to see why God allowed me to have polio.

Up until then, I had always purposely stayed away from people with disabilities. I didn't want to be associated with them. I didn't want to be around them because I was trying to pretend I wasn't handicapped; I was kind of running away from my own identity and my painful past. After I turned the corner, I made it a point to *approach* them, try to become friends with them, and share what God was doing in my life.

God is so patient with me. My favorite Scripture verse became Ephesians 2:10, which I used at the beginning of this chapter and also at the opening of this book: *"For we are His workmanship, created in Christ Jesus for good works, which God prepared beforehand that we should walk in them."*

Seeing my life in the light of this truth made a huge difference. We each have a purpose in life—even a throwaway kid with polio. Without it, I would just be trying to achieve one selfish goal after another until I died, always asking, "What's next? Now what?" I used to feel that if I didn't keep moving, I would die. Now I could rest in Him and follow His instructions. He would position me, and He would give me what I needed to do His work. He would keep me going on a straight path, even though I was still handicapped not only in body but also in spirit and soul. With Him, every morning would be a new beginning!

At last, I knew that nothing could separate me from His love, not even my own willfulness or ignorance. A verse from the letter Paul wrote to the Romans still resonates with my spirit:

> *"For I am convinced that neither death nor life, neither angels nor demons, neither the present nor the future, nor any powers, neither height nor depth, nor anything else in all creation, will be able to separate us from the love of God that is in Christ Jesus our Lord."*
>
> (Romans 8:38–39 NIV)

What really matters is how you handle your life, not the circumstances. So even if you're really old or physically impaired to the point that you can hardly do anything, your life still has meaning. Now I not only know where I'm going to spend eternity, but I know what to do before I die. I ask Him what to do and when and how. I follow Him. He helps me to be His wholehearted disciple. Once I have put myself into His hands, He has me. Nobody can snatch me out of His hands, not even the devil himself. Even if I lose all my faculties, He remains my Lord and Savior forever!

Once in California, I got a glimpse of what my life could have been like without the Lord Jesus. I was with a Chinese doctor and he asked if I would come to visit his brother, who had cerebral palsy and lived in a home for the disabled, where he had his own room. He could speak, but only with difficulty. I told him a little about my story, but I had to stop because he got very angry. "Why do *I* get cerebral palsy? My brother is a successful doctor with a beautiful wife, beautiful children, and a nice house—while I am trapped in this body!"

I tried to tell him what I had gone through, but he didn't want to hear it. He got so upset, he tried to ram me with his wheelchair. "Get outta here! I don't wanna hear about Jesus! I'm mad at Him. That's *your* story. I don't wanna hear you. Don't tell me about Jesus. If He was loving, He wouldn't have done this to me...." We had to leave, and I never found out what happened to him after that. There, but for the very real grace of God, go I.

NEW STEVE, NEW RESPONSIBILITIES

Sook Hee was glad she had listened when the Lord said she should become my shadow. Her "new" husband made quite a few changes at home, and she was happy to comply. To start with, I took time to pray and read the Bible first thing in the morning. In the evening, I would gather the family together for another time of prayer. I continued to work hard during the day, but I began to learn how to keep my work from dominating my existence.

My job changed again, too. In 1996, I was recruited by ConAgra Functional Foods as vice president of marketing and sales. Once again, we packed up and moved, this time from Evansville, Indiana, to Omaha, Nebraska.

My experience with Mead Johnson's Boost nutritional drink helped with my new role, which involved relicensing the patented probiotic LGG so that it could be incorporated into nutritional products in the United States.[13] Worldwide rights to LGG had been sold to a Finnish dairy company called Valio, headquartered in Helsinki, and I was part of a leadership team to help market new functional food products with LGG in the U.S. At first, we put it into capsules that

13. LGG stands for Lactobacillus [rhamnosus] GG. The "GG" comes from the last names of the two doctors at Tufts University who discovered the bacterial strain in 1985, Dr. Sherwood Gorbach and Dr. Barry Goldin. Probiotics promote the growth of beneficial bacteria in people's intestines and help to restore intestinal balance after antibiotic use, yeast infections, "traveler's diarrhea," and the like.

were sold at drugstores, and we were hoping to put it into foods such as yogurt. We created the brand name, "Culturelle with LGG," since the name "LGG" was already a registered trademark. Ultimately, the brand Culturelle got sold by ConAgra, which marked the end of my assignment.

In the meantime, we got involved in a new church in Omaha, Westside Baptist. Early on, Sook Hee signed me up for Bible Study Fellowship (BSF), and to tell the truth, I was not too happy about it. "We just moved—new job, new city. I really don't have time for it."

But her response was simple, "That is *why* you need this Bible study." She was right. As it turned out, the teaching leader of the men's BSF also had polio, which I couldn't have known ahead of time. Before long, I was made a group leader, and in that capacity, I would grow spiritually in ways that I could not on my own.

Sometimes, the growth proved to be humorous. Early on, I was told that as long as I was a BSF group leader, I should not drink alcoholic beverages, lest I lead people the wrong way. The pastor, Tony Lambert, preached about it, telling stories about when he was younger and used to drink and run around. My son Richard, who was in middle school, heard that and he took me to task: "Dad, you're not supposed to drink!"

"I'm not supposed to get drunk and I never do," I countered. "But it's okay to have alcohol around the house." I never drank that much anyway. There are many instances in the Bible warning people not to get drunk. First Peter 5:8 says, *"Be alert and of sober mind. Your enemy the devil prowls around like a roaring lion looking for someone to devour"* (NIV). But the Bible does not say we need to abstain from alcohol.

Richard persisted. "But the pastor said, 'Do not drink!'"

So I took all of the alcohol in the house—some of which was fairly expensive stuff—and poured it down the drain for Richard to see. "Okay, Richard." The old Steve would never have done that.

Another time, I was teaching the ten-week introductory class at church. There I was, a short Korean guy with leg braces, co-leading with this big football player. We made quite a pair. The church, being Baptist, believed in full-immersion baptism, but neither one of us had been baptized that way. How were we supposed to stand up and say it was the only way to go, when we hadn't done it ourselves? My excuse, of course, was that I hadn't wanted to get my braces wet the first time, so I had been baptized by sprinkling. But in this context, that excuse fell a bit flat.

While I remained on the fence about baptism, we went as a family to Breckenridge, Colorado, where a friend had offered us the use of her condo. While we were there, I went white-water rafting and wore waders to protect my expensive braces. It was a wild trip and I held on tight with both hands the whole way. Then at the end of the trip, the water got calm and I relaxed. Hanging on with only one hand, I was sitting in the back when the raft suddenly hit a rock. I have no balance anyway, and the impact tossed me overboard into the river. My waders filled up immediately with ice-cold water, and I took a quick breath before I began to sink. As I went down, I remember looking up and praying, "Lord, get me out of here and I will get baptized by full immersion!" I could see people looking over at me through the clear water. Once my waders sort of equalized, the guide was able to pull me up and out. It took only about thirty seconds, but it seemed like an eternity.

Back in Omaha the following week, I told our class what had happened and that I was going to get baptized by immersion as soon as possible. My co-leader said he would do it, too. In fact, everyone in the class got baptized. This time, I didn't have to worry about my braces because the baptism was not going to be held in a lake. I could take them off ahead of time and just scoot myself to the edge of the baptismal pool at the church.

SOOK HEE TAKES A MISSION ASSIGNMENT

In the meantime, Sook Hee got involved with the church's mission outreaches. She was in charge of collecting personal care items, toys, diapers, and other supplies from the congregation. She sorted and inventoried them and then accompanied the denomination's dental and medical mission teams when they went to Nicaragua.

This put her into an unfamiliar role of speaking (through a translator) about the gospel to groups of people. The Nicaraguan street kids had never seen Asians. They would call out to her, saying, 'Chino! Chino!" Unlike me, Sook Hee ordinarily has a great fear of public speaking. But there in Nicaragua, her fear vanished as she spoke to the kids. She often told my story as well as her own, and she found that my story made a big impact on the listeners.

"I feel that it's my job to tell Steve's story," she says. "It is all right with me to be his 'shadow.' Even though my life is interesting, too, people react more to his story, and it helps bring people to Christ."

The mission team came up with unique ways to get the gospel message out. For example, once after they had preached, some gang members started hanging around. Security guards tried to wave them away, but Sook Hee said, "No, bring them closer. They need to hear about God, too." Then she took some Lucky Charms cereal, which they had never seen before, mixed it with some popcorn, and poured it into a big bowl, inviting them to help themselves to the colorful snack. While they munched, Sook Hee shared my testimony with the help of her very good translator, and at the end, all of the gang members, about ten of them, accepted Christ.

NEW ROLE BRINGS MORE STRESS

Once Culturelle was launched, I was shifted into a new role that involved reporting to ConAgra's Food Division via weekly travel between Omaha and Fulton, California. This significant amount of travelling proved to be very stressful, both for me and my family. My absence during the week was especially hard on Sook Hee and the children. This traveling went on for seven months with no end in sight, so I resigned. It was 1999 and I joined AmeriTrade, an online stock brokerage based in Omaha, as vice president of marketing acquisition and retention. The job did not involve any travel and we would not have to move again.

Marketing stocks was quite a switch from selling nutritional products. I enjoyed the work initially. In fact, I came up with a brilliant marketing scheme that I learned from consumer package marketing, and it worked very well: we would give people an incentive to sign up with the company—thirty free trades. Previously, they used to make a big deal out of their per-trade prices, but that didn't give people any reason to drop everything and do it right then. But when we began to say, "Just open an account today, and we will give you thirty free trades in your first thirty days," they acted on it. Boom; it just took off, and my superiors were very pleased. However, after a while, I began to see that although my idea created a lot of business for AmeriTrade—it was so successful, we signed up one million accounts in less than a year—it was very bad for the people who got hooked. Some became day traders. I had people sending me emails saying, "I can't stop trading. Help me! I need professional help."

It was also very bad for me and my family because I had become such a slave to the stock market. I was making more money than ever before, but at what cost? What is money when your life is getting sucked out of you? Sook Hee would turn on the TV every afternoon to see how the stock market had performed that day, and she would tell Richard and Racheal about it before I got home. That is, if I got home.

I lived and worked in Nebraska, but I couldn't get free of California. With ConAgra, I had to fly to California all of the time. Now, I couldn't leave work until the end of the workday for our West Coast customers, which meant that often I didn't get home until 9 p.m. I worked day and night, even sometimes on Saturdays. I rarely had a weekend off. I didn't sleep well. I often skipped meals. Once I had to go to the emergency room because my heart rate was so elevated. Sook Hee kept asking me to quit for my health's sake.

I was on the verge of quitting when the decision was made for me. Over-speculation involving the rapidly growing number of Internet-based companies had inflated the Nasdaq composite stock market index, which peaked in value in March 2000. Then the "dot.com bubble" began to burst, taking down a large number of companies and investors' portfolios over the next few months and, in fact, over the next couple of years. A lot of people lost their jobs—including me, in August 2000.

I was free! Sook Hee was so happy. The other women in her Bible study group were worried about the whole thing, but not her.

She says, "When Steve came home at 4:00 in the afternoon and said, 'I've lost my job,' I jumped up and down and threw out my arms and said, 'Congratulations! Hallelujah!"

Because I was laid off, I got a severance package, so I did not have to find a new position immediately. I was just at home. No longer did Sook Hee and the kids have to compete with my job. This made it possible for us to reconnect with each other as a family; it was one of the best stretches of time we'd ever had. Looking back, it became obvious that God had His hand on every detail of what had just happened and He was going to use it to launch me on the next exciting installment of my life story.

10

BEGINNING AGAIN

For this reason we also, since the day we heard it, do not cease to pray for you, and to ask that you may be filled with the knowledge of His will in all wisdom and spiritual understanding; that you may walk worthy of the Lord, fully pleasing Him, being fruitful in every good work and increasing in the knowledge of God; strengthened with all might, according to His glorious power, for all patience and longsuffering with joy; giving thanks to the Father who has qualified us to be partakers of the inheritance of the saints in the light. He has delivered us from the power of darkness and conveyed us into the kingdom of the Son of His love, in whom we have redemption through His blood, the forgiveness of sins.

—Colossians 1:9–14

Song Kyung Soo was smiling at me from his electric wheelchair, so I smiled back. Sook Hee and I were back in Korea, standing next to Harry Holt's grave on top of a hill overlooking the Holt orphanage in Ilsan, where I had lived forty years before. The three of us had just attended the funeral of Grandma Bertha Holt, where we had both delivered eulogies, his in Korean and mine in English.

"Song, do you remember me?" I asked, able only to recollect the family name of my childhood friend.

With difficulty because of his cerebral palsy, Song Kyung Soo replied and Sook Hee translated. "Myung Soo, of course I remember you. You used to beat me up all the time."

I was mortified…but it was true. I used to take out my frustrations on Song Kyung Soo, who was helpless to defend himself. Boys who were not handicapped would make me the victim of their taunts and beatings during the school day, and then I would come back to the orphanage, swing into our room like a raging lion, and give Kyung Soo a pounding. In fact, I was often so angry about being picked on at school that I would line up all of the kids, both boys and girls, who were more disabled than I was, and give each of them a beating. What a horrible way to be remembered! I felt so bad for what I did to those helpless kids.

"Oh, Kyung Soo, I am so, so sorry." I wanted to vanish. "Can you ever forgive me for what I did?"

He smiled again. "Myung Soo, I forgave you a long time ago because Jesus forgave me for my sins."

I was speechless. Here was a man so trapped in his body that he could barely feed himself. Instead of doing all of the normal things a man can do—going to school, getting a job, getting married, having kids—he was still living in the same orphanage, which had been turned into a facility for handicapped adults. And he was content, happy, and free of resentment. He said he had been a Christian for only about six years. He had his Bible in the back of his wheelchair.

For so many years, I had blocked out those painful memories. Now I had to deal with them and face my past cruelty.

(Miraculously, Kyung Soo has since gotten married and, with assistance, now lives in a home of his own.)

I came away from this encounter sobered and pensive. God had forgiven me for everything I ever did wrong. I could never repay Him. Why had He given me so much? What was I doing with all of His gifts? Was it right just to keep piling up money and status for myself? Perhaps I should reconsider the direction of my life.

MORE BLESSED TO GIVE THAN TO RECEIVE

That was August 2000, and I had come back to Korea to attend the funeral of Grandma Holt, who had passed away in July. I had come because I was a member of the U.S. board of directors for Holt International Children's Services. Also, having just been laid off by AmeriTrade, I had plenty of time to make a trip to attend a funeral in another country. Using some of the air miles accrued from my corporate travel, Sook Hee and I had made the trip together, leaving our young teens with friends.

The funeral had been one long, amazing outpouring of affection and respect for Grandma Holt. A thousand people had attended, including the first lady of Korea, Lee Hui-ho. It was like a state funeral. When Bertha Holt's casket had arrived at the airport, they had closed off all the roads along the way, and a police-escorted motorcade had transported it all the way to the orphanage in Ilsan, where she would be buried next to her husband, Harry. Grandma Holt had made a huge impact on Korea because of her care for war babies and ongoing work among the helpless and homeless orphans. She had never retired from her work, even after she had moved back to Oregon and had handed off to others all of the responsibilities for the wide-ranging Holt network of childcare centers and adoption programs. Through it all, her Christian faith shone its light on her path. Like her husband before her, she had given her all to others. In 1966, President Lyndon B. Johnson had named Bertha Holt Mother of the Year. In 1995, she had become the only non-Korean ever to receive the Korea National Merit Award. Her legacy was impressive and admirable.

I was one of her success stories. I had started with so little and had been given so very much in life. Since making Jesus my Lord, I had made an extra effort to give back to others, and that was part of the reason I had agreed to serve on the board for Holt. For years, Sook Hee had sponsored children through World Vision International, the Christian humanitarian aid organization. We had worked with church teams to reach out to others. But the bulk of my time was spent working harder than any other corporate executive I knew, amassing my personal wealth. I had bought and sold homes and had acquired driver's licenses in half a dozen states. I had achieved super-platinum frequent-flyer status. I was determined to provide my two children with the finest education that money could buy. I was generous in giving my time to my church.

But the fact is, I was running like a hamster on a wheel, going nowhere with all my might, which is a pretty crazy thing for a guy with paralyzed legs to say.

"Myung Soo, I forgave you a long time ago because Jesus forgave me for my sins."

Kyung Soo's words had a powerful effect on me. Back home in Omaha, I started praying about them. *What should I do with the rest of my life, Lord?* I took extra time to think and recharge. I realized I was at a transition point and I wanted God's guidance for the future. At our church, I signed up for a thirteen-week course called "Experiencing God," based on the book of the same name by Henry Blackaby. I learned about the idea of seeing where God is working and then joining Him instead of starting your own good works.

What did that mean in my case? Eventually, without urgency, I started looking for employment. Since I was accustomed to the corporate world, I contacted my headhunters. One of them got me a series of interviews with Hallmark, which is headquartered in Kansas City, not far from Omaha, for the position of head of new business development. I didn't get the job, although I was the first runner-up. But they said, "In six months, we're going to have a new division, and we think we'd rather have you in that position."

In the meantime, I had become reacquainted with the history of Holt International. On the long flight home from Grandma Holt's funeral, I had read all the way through her book about the history of Holt, *The Seed from the East*. Until then, I had not realized that Bob Pierce, the founder of World Vision, had played a significant role in the founding of Holt. That gave me the idea for something radical. I did some research on the Internet, and then I cold-called the senior vice president of marketing and sales (my area of expertise) to see if they had any marketing positions open at World Vision. This was a bold thing to do, yet I seemed to have placed the call at just the right time.

The senior vice president, Atul Tandon, answered the phone. "Hello...I don't usually pick up my phone. I don't know why I picked it up this time."

"Because God told you to pick it up," I replied.

"Who is this?!" he asked.

"This is Steve Stirling...." and I told him why I was calling, giving him a little background.

He told me he was about to leave for India on an earthquake relief mission, but he would see me when he got back.

I should add that I was not completely unemployed during this time. I had taken on a couple of contract jobs to fill the few months before I could land another "real" job. One was developing marketing for an Omaha organization called Income Dynamics before their software was sold to Intuit, which incorporated ItsDeductible as a free tool in their TurboTax programs. The other was working with a private Christian institution of higher education in Omaha called Grace University, helping to rebrand the school and refocus their strategic direction.

It felt good to be using my skills to help people. I had always liked the idea of doing so, although the fact that most of the products I had marketed over the years were designed to help people had never caused me to consider switching to nonprofit management for an organization such as World Vision. As far as I knew, no other executive had ever made such a switch. I had admired leaders of nonprofits for their altruism and creativity, but I'd admired savvy corporate leaders more.

After Atul Tandon returned from his trip, he arranged an interview with World Vision. It went very well, although they didn't have an opening for a vice president of marketing. I told them, "I will do anything you want me to do. It's not about me. I'm trying to see what God wants me to do." After further interviews, they offered me a job in Federal Way, Washington, as vice president of marketing operations. Later, I would become executive director of major donor fundraising for World Vision U.S. Clearly, God was in this.

I returned to Omaha and the very next day, I got a call from the headhunter who had put me in touch with Hallmark six months earlier. "Hallmark just called, and they want to offer you that job as VP/general manager of a division." This corporate position was my dream job, and it looked as though Sook Hee might also be able to work as an artist at Hallmark. But I had already said yes to the World Vision job.

I had to go to Grace University the next day to attend their once-a-week chapel service, and I saw a banner with John 4:35 on it: "*Do you think the work of harvesting will not begin until the summer ends four months from now? Look around you! Vast fields of human souls are ripening all around us, and are ready now for reaping*" (TLB).

I considered this a strong confirmation that working for World Vision was the right decision. God was saying to me, "The harvest fields need you *now*. Don't wait until you retire. My kingdom harvest won't wait. Do it now."

Sook Hee and I had been praying for God's will in our lives. We had prayed specifically, "Lord, please have the Hallmark position be offered first if that's the one you want us to accept." If they had called earlier, I would have jumped at that opportunity, without waiting for World Vision to call. And look what had happened: the Hallmark offer had come a scant twenty-four hours *after* the one from World Vision.

We started packing to move to Washington State.

MORE CONFIRMATION THIS WAS THE RIGHT MOVE

Before signing on the dotted line, we sat down with Richard and Racheal. Taking the World Vision job would reduce my income drastically, which carried big implications for their future education—and more. "Kids, I have two offers, and the one I think God wants me to take pays a whole lot less than the other one. We're thinking about your college education. Since the stock market crash in 2000, our college savings have not recovered well enough yet to send both of you to private universities at the same time, although we do have enough to send you to public universities. If I take the World Vision job, we won't be able to pay for more than an undergraduate degree at a public school."

In unison, they said, "Dad, we're okay with that." They understood that to attend a more expensive college, they would now have to get loans and scholarships to make up the difference. (This is what eventually happened, and things worked out very well for both of them). They were perfectly willing to make the adjustments necessary for our family to live on a smaller income. And they told us that they didn't mind moving again; in fact, they said all of our family moves had equipped them well for adult life by making them adaptable and open to new people and new experiences.

God's provision extended to the details of the move. It really showed me that when you seek the Lord with all your heart, mind, soul, and strength, He will take care of you, even in ways you can't anticipate. When He calls you to go somewhere new, He will guide you and equip you. The moving process could have been quite worrisome. Although we were old pros at it after nineteen years, this move would be different. In the corporate world, the new company picks up your realtor fee, your closing costs, moving costs—everything. You actually make money when you move because they pay for so much. If your old house doesn't sell right away, they get two appraisals for it and hand you a check for the average amount so you don't have to worry about selling your house. World Vision offered to pay for our move—with a cap—but not for all of our other expenses. They were offering a much lower salary, too, and we would be moving to a much more expensive area.

Just before I got the job offer from World Vision, we had planned to host a birthday party for Sook Hee and another church member, but an ice storm had postponed it until after the job offer came through. Our guests did not know that we were going to have to sell our house, so I was surprised when one of the party guests started looking it over.

I asked him if he was interested in our house, and he answered, "Yeah, I'm looking to buy a place."

It was a three-story, five-thousand-square-foot house, not counting the walk-out basement. He worked for a software company and it suited his needs perfectly. To make a long story short, he ended up buying our house. He even wanted the baby grand piano, which meant we wouldn't have to move it. So we sold the house with no hassle and no realtor fees. He gave us the appraised value, and we didn't even have to list it. It was the answer to a prayer request we hadn't even had a chance to make. When I told the people at World Vision about it, they found it hard to believe.

PROVIDENTIAL DETAILS, UNIQUE OPPORTUNITIES

Moving to World Vision thrust me into a new, nonprofit business world, and yet I found multiple ways in which God had been in the details of my jobs with for-profit companies. This became even more obvious later as I branched out and worked for more nonprofits. My new world focused more on building up God's kingdom rather than building up profits. Money was secondary to mission. Helping people overcome poverty or nutritional and health problems is more important than taking advantage of them by selling them products they might not need.

I looked back with amazement at my nineteen years of corporate jobs, which only God knew would equip me so perfectly for what was to come. For example, even back when I worked for McNeil, I was learning how to help children and adults with new products that were safe from negative side effects. When I worked for Mead-Johnson the first time, I learned what it took to create wholesome baby food, and when I worked for them the second time, I learned about nutritional products for adults. With Jobst, I learned that not all medical problems involve drugs, and special equipment is just as important. Working for

ConAgra, I not only learned about probiotics, but I learned about what we now call "functional foods," foods that help to maximize your health. While I was there, they developed a barley flour called Sustagrain that had a low glycemic index, but was very high-fiber and satiating, thus good for diabetics. I would never have known much about such things without that job.

I also learned (the hard way) what to avoid if I intended to serve God and other people. My brief stint as an AmeriTrade marketer had hurt me, my family, and the people I convinced to trade too much. In contrast, consulting for Grace University helped to smooth my transition from the corporate world to the nonprofit world. Helping equip future Christian leaders was much more appropriate for a dedicated, Christ-following business leader.

The more I explored my new role, the more I appreciated God's provision. Certainly it was God's hand that brought me from destitution in Korea to the United States of America, where I found so many opportunities. Here, not only could I receive advanced medical care and enhanced handicap accessibility, I also could expect to move freely into positions of leadership, unimpeded by my humble background or ethnicity. Where else but in the United States could a polio-afflicted orphan achieve so much?

How good it proved to be that I had come from such a deprived background. My new job would take me more than once to Mexico City, where I encountered street kids. One time, I visited some boys who lived in the sewers. When they saw my crutches, they said, "Why are you here?"

My response was simple: "I want to share with you that Jesus loves you."

A street-tough boy named Sergio countered with, "No. Jesus does not love me. I do bad things." We talked about Jesus's forgiveness and love, but he didn't seem to be convinced. When I got up to go, Sergio offered me something as a gift: a small beetle. I took it and held it carefully. Then he said, "Since you accepted my gift, I will accept yours." And he prayed the prayer of salvation.

Another time, I talked about God's love with a group of girls in a Mexico City halfway house. There were three girls in this group who had been street kids, and besides the clothing on their backs, the only possession each of them had was a stuffed animal. At the conclusion of our visit, they said, "Sir, we want to give you our teddy bears so you will remember that we love you, too." I was so moved and humbled. They were giving me the only things they owned. We still have them. I was poor like that once.

Although it is never easy for me to travel, especially to fly, I recognized that God had preserved me from worse debilitation so that I could do it. To this day, I must get on and off airplanes by myself, take care of personal needs in cramped quarters, climb stairs, solve unusual problems, and endure lengthy discomforts. But my abundant experience with long-distance travel, combined with my gratitude for every opportunity to serve, enables me to continue doing it.

MEETING MY SPONSOR, AUNT BEULAH

Early on, after starting at World Vision, I discovered my name, Cho Myung Soo, on their lists of sponsored children. Much to my amazement, I also found that my sponsor had been none other than the sister of Grandma Bertha Holt, Beulah Holt Stronczek.

Apparently, she had obtained my name directly from her niece, Molly Holt. The first Ilsan orphan that Aunt Beulah had sponsored through World Vision was so sick that she died. So Aunt Beulah told her niece, "Molly, this time will you get me a kid who won't die on me?" Molly figured she'd pick the orneriest kid—me. "You can sponsor Myung Soo. The ornery ones don't die." That's how Aunt Beulah got me. She sent support money until I left the orphanage, and she prayed for me for years. Her generosity may have provided me with my first crutches.

She lived in Walla Walla, Washington, and we got in touch with her. First, she came to our house and she was amazed that it was so nice. "This is your *house?*" she asked. Then we went to visit her. It was humbling because she lived in a double-wide trailer.

She told us that when she was sponsoring me back in the sixties, her husband was working for the post office, and they didn't have a lot of money. He told her, "If you want to sponsor that handicapped kid in Korea, you'll have to find your own money because I don't want to send $10 a month."

She said, "Okay, I will clean houses." So she cleaned people's houses to sponsor me. When she told me she used to pray for me, I was thinking, *Oh, she must have prayed that I'd get adopted by an American family, get a job, get a wife....* But instead, she said, "I prayed that one day, you would come to know the Lord."

That has got to be one of the biggest reasons that I did come to know the Lord. Otherwise, it doesn't make sense that Sook Hee and I are still pretty much the only Christians in our families. Because of Aunt Beulah's faithfulness, we came to Christ. Apart from her, there are only three other women I know of who prayed for me: my mother, my aunt, and my Christian stepmother in Korea.

SINGING A SONG

Through Holt International, I found out that my friend, Song Kyung Soo, was coming to Oregon to perform with a Holt children's choir. That was an unexpected blessing for all of us. We went to the performance, and we took the whole group out to dinner in a restaurant afterward. This provided a perfect opportunity for us to introduce him to our two children.

Kyung Soo and I marveled at the way God had taken care of both of us. While most people would have relegated us to the trash heap of life, God had other plans. He healed our hearts and made us whole. He knew what He would do to redeem our broken lives and use us for His glory.

Although Kyung Soo has never been healed from his cerebral palsy, and I have never been healed from the aftereffects of polio, it makes me think of Jesus's story about the man who was born blind:

> *As He passed by, He saw a man blind from birth. And His disciples asked Him, "Rabbi, who sinned, this man or his parents, that he would be born blind?" Jesus answered, "It was neither that this man sinned, nor his parents; but it was so that the works of God might be displayed in him. We must work the works of Him who sent Me as long as it is day; night is coming when no one can work. While I am in the world, I am the Light of the world." When He had said this, He spat on the ground, and made clay of the spittle, and applied the clay to his eyes, and said to him, "Go, wash in the pool of Siloam" (which is translated, Sent). So he went away and washed, and came back seeing.* (John 9:1–7 NASB)

Who sinned? Our Korean parents? Our grandparents? We ourselves, Kyung Soo and Myung Soo? It doesn't matter because everyone has sinned. What matters is that God brought us out of spiritual blindness and into His brilliant light—for His glory!

11

FULL OF ANTICIPATION

For You will light my lamp; the Lord my God will enlighten my darkness. For by You I can run against a troop, by my God I can leap over a wall. As for God, His way is perfect; the word of the Lord is proven; He is a shield to all who trust in Him. For who is God, except the Lord? And who is a rock, except our God? It is God who arms me with strength, and makes my way perfect.

—Psalm 18:28–32

In India, even moderately priced hotels have a lot of marble in them, which makes everything quite elegant—and potentially very slippery underfoot.

I had been invited by World Vision India to come to Madurai to visit their polio homes for girls and boys. I was traveling and staying in a hotel by myself. The night before my visit to the polio home, I took a bath. To keep from having to rush in the morning, I always take baths or showers the night before. A little puddle of water on the bathroom's marble floor made me slip and fall. I could tell that I had hurt my ankle pretty badly, so I crawled back to my bed and called the front desk.

"Please call my World Vision host and tell him to come." He and some others came and took me to the emergency room in a wheelchair, where they X-rayed my rapidly-swelling ankle. It was not broken, but it was very badly sprained.

They sent me back to the hotel with instructions to rest in bed with my ankle propped up for three or four days, in hopes that the swelling would diminish enough to permit me to put on my brace and my shoes so I could get around on my crutches. The visit to the polio home would have to be postponed until my ankle was better.

The first day wasn't too bad, but after a while, there's only so much Bollywood you can watch. So I turned off the TV and began to think and pray. Pondering my upcoming visit to the polio home, my thoughts turned to my own experiences living with the other disabled children in the Ilsan orphanage. We were housed and cared for by a succession of adults, yet I did not remember one single *hug* during my entire four years in the orphanage. That took me aback.

I had fond memories of the next best thing—being carried around on the shoulders of G.I.s who would come at Christmastime from the American base and entertain us for a while. But no hugs. Well, I did remember one single hug when I was in the army hospital for surgery, and I didn't know what was going on. I'd had a very painful shot that made me cry, quietly. A nurse came over and hugged me. That was the only hug I received in four years!

What must it be like for the young people I was about to visit?

"THINK ABOUT WHOSE YOU ARE"

God began to speak to me in that hotel room. He said something like this, *"Instead of thinking, 'I am the vice president of World Vision and I'm coming here to help disabled kids,' think about who you belong to—Me."*

In other words, "Don't think about *who* you are. Instead, think about *whose* you are."

That idea took hold in me.

When at last, about a week later, I was able to purchase some compression stockings so that I could get my black-and-blue foot inside my shoe, the timing was perfect for my visit to the two children's homes—much better than it would have been a week earlier. It was Palm Sunday—and also Polio Vaccination Day. It was well worth being waylaid by my painful injury. Had I come a week earlier, none of the following would have happened.

The residents of the polio home had heard that this Korean-American guy who used to live in a home like theirs was coming to visit them. When I arrived, they were all waiting for me, lined up, as if they were welcoming me home—reminiscent of the way Jesus was welcomed into Jerusalem on the first Palm Sunday. Some were in wobbly wheelchairs, some were standing, and some were sitting on the floor. I went around, shook their hands, and then I sat down on the floor, too. They surrounded me and touched me; I reached out and hugged each one of them. Then we gathered together for a special worship service.

Afterward, I was able to go out with a team and help to administer the oral polio vaccine to the young children who lived in the vicinity. I wanted to give these kids what I wished I could have had—a simple, safe vaccine that can prevent so much suffering. And a hug. There I was, sitting in a chair, surrounded by smiling kids. They hugged me as I hugged every one of them back.

World Vision India, like many organizations, is staffed chiefly by people without disabilities. I was driven to their new headquarters in Chennai, where I had been invited to give my testimony at their weekly devotion time, which was held in the only room large enough to accommodate all of the staff members—on the very top floor.

Even as they were actively participating in the polio eradication efforts and helping to establish the homes for young people who had contracted the disease, they had not considered physical disabilities when they built their new building. They had neglected to put an elevator in the sleek, new, five-story building. Wide steps led to an inviting entrance behind a heavy glass door; inside, a single stairwell led to the floors above. How was I going to do this?

At first, it appeared to be impossible, but I decided to climb up all of those flights of stairs so that I could give the talk—and so I could make a point about their need for an elevator. It was hot and I was pretty sweaty by the time I got to the top. But I told my story—which had more impact because I had just climbed those stairs with so much difficulty. Then before I went back down, I made my plea: "Please consider adding an elevator to this building so that people like me can come in!"

Then, as now, I occupy a unique position: a senior executive for a nonprofit charity that provides for children in needy places…and I myself came from the same kind of background. Merely by showing up, I can be an advocate for others with handicaps and a living testimonial to the importance of preventive measures such as the polio vaccine.

THE BLESSINGS OF MY WORLD VISION YEARS

The four and a half years I worked for World Vision couldn't have been better in terms of personal fulfillment and family cohesiveness. Living in the Seattle area put us only one flight away from my parents and Sook Hee's widowed mother in Anchorage; we had never been so close before.

My suitability for the job was obvious. World Vision is about helping needy children, and the fact that I had been in a disadvantaged situation in Korea meant that I could relate to them. I could speak on behalf of children in crisis, and I knew what I was talking about. Besides, World Vision had always supported a lot of Korean kids, so my Korean heritage made me a good fit, too. I could speak to the reality of being destitute, and I could talk about what it's like to live without any possessions, totally dependent upon others, which is not a good feeling because people prefer to be self-sufficient. I could present a good case for meeting their needs in innovative ways that provide dignity for the aid recipients. I knew that people don't want to be needy forever.

There, I also learned that the world of Christian nonprofit charities is not picture-perfect because it is populated with human beings like everywhere else, albeit sinners saved by grace. I had naïvely thought that all Christians should always get along without friction, humming "Kumbaya, My Lord" throughout their workdays.

Of course, that is not true. This workplace, like any church, was full of human interactions that revealed subtle sins such as pride—sometimes, even pride in one's self-sacrifice and care for others. Just because we all worked for a Christian international non-governmental organization (INGO) did not make us perfectly virtuous! This was a good thing for me to recognize.

While I was working for World Vision, Richard went off to college, leaving just three of us at home. Racheal was a senior in high school. When I was recruited by an organization called Childhelp in Scottsdale, Arizona, Sook Hee and Racheal stayed in Washington State for several months so that Racheal could finish high school there while I found a house in Arizona. For nine months, I only saw them about once a month.

FIGHTING A DIFFERENT FIGHT

I served as senior vice president of marketing and resource development at Childhelp, which works to rescue and help children who have been abused physically or sexually and traumatized psychologically. Childhelp operates programs in California and Arizona. Although the organization now works primarily with families and children who live in the United States, its founders began their work among Japanese "throwaway kids" during the Korean War.

This gave me a curious connection. Although I had never been sexually abused myself, in most respects, I could certainly identify with any children who were being neglected and taken advantage of by adults, and I could throw myself into the charitable efforts of my new employers. Among other things, I learned the simple fact that it's not only kids from faraway countries who need assistance, but also American children. In addition to requiring physical assistance and protection, they are often living with psychological and emotional damage that needs to be addressed. Along the way, I learned some things about myself and how, through Christ, healing can be achieved.

During the two years I worked for Childhelp, it became more important to move back north again. My father died of lung and pancreatic cancer, leaving my mother a widow. I actually tried (and failed) to find a job in Anchorage so I could be close to her.

One day, I fell and injured myself in the auditorium in Phoenix. A friend invited me to sample some pain-relieving products that worked remarkably well, and I learned that the company that made them, Univera, was located in Lacey, Washington. Eventually, I took a job with Univera. It was good to be able to return to a place so much closer to Alaska. However, the job thrust me back into the corporate world, where I discovered that I was not happy anymore.

Fortunately, my unhappiness did not last long. After only eight months, I was laid off due to the subprime mortgage crisis and resulting global financial crisis of September 2008. Now, in all likelihood, we were not going to be able to live in the Pacific Northwest anymore.

JOINING HEIFER INTERNATIONAL

Looking for a way back to the nonprofit environment, I signed on with Heifer International, and we moved to Little Rock, Arkansas, where their headquarters is located. As its name indicates, this organization provides animal husbandry assistance to needy people in other countries. They are guided by the motto of their founder, Dan West, who was distributing cups of milk to people in a poverty-stricken country when he realized how much more helpful and sustainable it would be to provide the whole cow instead. Heifer's outreach now extends across the globe to four continents.

Right from the start, in the midst of the global recession, I had to make unpopular decisions as the executive vice president of resource development. Circumstances necessitated cutting down on staff and redundant functions. Along with other expense cuts, we closed many regional offices, and we expanded the distribution of our holiday gift catalog, which is how most people find out about the work of Heifer and how most of the donations come in.

Every job provides an education, and this one was no exception. During the three years that I worked there, I not only resumed international travel, but I learned much about how to reach out to people—in this case, mostly disadvantaged women—and empower them through agricultural assistance, which improves their quality of life in tangible, sustainable ways.

RECRUITED BY CHILDFUND INTERNATIONAL

After three years, we moved once more, this time to Richmond, Virginia, on the East Coast, a significant step closer to where we are today. I had been recruited as executive vice president and chief administrative officer of ChildFund International, a move up the corporate ladder in the nonprofit sphere. ChildFund coordinates the sponsorship of vulnerable children in thirty countries around the world, including the United States. Networked with partner organizations, ChildFund also helps to coordinate aid projects to the communities the children live in. The biggest part of their work consists of monthly donations from individual child sponsors, who are connected to the children they sponsor by means of personal correspondence.

Not long before I came on board, the organization had changed its name from the Christian Children's Fund to ChildFund. Although it had been founded as a Christian outreach, and there were still a lot of Christians working there, they wanted to become more inclusive of other religions. They did not want to offend people in predominantly non-Christian countries or in the United States at their Richmond headquarters. However, many of their longtime supporters reacted negatively to this name change and decided to take their sponsorships elsewhere once they completed their obligations to the children with whom they had developed ties.

As with my positions at other organizations, particularly the ones in the nonprofit sector, working with ChildFund entailed international travel. Recently, I tallied up the countries that I have been privileged to visit during my adult life—fifty-eight out of one hundred and ninety-five countries in the world today. Some of them I have visited more than once. Not bad for a kid on crutches who was confined to a Korean orphanage for four years!

A BETTER MAP THAN GPS

In each of the positions I occupied with the nonprofit organizations, I learned much that was new and applied it. Sook Hee and I grew in our Christian lives even as Richard and Racheal grew up and moved on to colleges and careers. Along the way, I made every effort to obey God, do right by others, and live out of my new life in Christ. He had become the center of my focus and I was willing to pull up stakes and follow Him wherever He might lead.

We had been in Richmond for three years and we liked living there. But one day, a recruiter called on behalf of Medical Assistance Programs (MAP) International, an organization based in Georgia. She was looking specifically for someone who could step into the role of president and CEO there, someone with the leadership qualities who was also a strong Christian. MAP International wanted a person with plenty of business experience as well as INGO experience. The organization provided life-saving medicines and medical supplies to people in other countries who would not have it otherwise—children in particular. It would be a bonus if they could find someone who possessed not only the basic qualifications they desired, but who also could identify with the people they served.

Would this Korean-American candidate—who'd had polio and whose résumé was packed with senior executive experience—be interested?

12

BY DIVINE APPOINTMENT

Blessed be the God and Father of our Lord Jesus Christ, who has blessed us with every spiritual blessing in the heavenly places in Christ, just as He chose us in Him before the foundation of the world, that we would be holy and blameless before Him. In love He predestined us to adoption as sons through Jesus Christ to Himself, according to the kind intention of His will, to the praise of the glory of His grace, which He freely bestowed on us in the Beloved.

—Ephesians 1:3–6 (NASB)

We have a perfect job for you as president and CEO of a nonprofit," the recruiter had said.

"What nonprofit?" I asked.

"MAP."

"Who uses a map? Everyone uses GPS."

She clarified, "No, it's not about maps. It stands for Medical Assistance Programs."

I was not interested and I told her so.

That evening, I told Sook Hee about the call. "What did you tell them?" she asked.

"I said no because I told ChildFund I will commit to their organization for at least three to five years, and I've only been here two and a half. Also, I doubt I'm qualified."

Sook Hee gently reminded me that for my whole life, God had been preparing me for a senior role like this. She cited my personal life experiences in the orphanage and with polio, my work for corporate pharmaceutical companies such as Johnson & Johnson and Bristol-Myers Squibb, and my years of working for nonprofits such as World Vision.

"Aren't you going to at least pray about it?" she asked. "They're a Christian organization. What if God wants you to go there?"

She was right to exert a little pressure. Together, we prayed on the spot.

My attitude began to shift. Maybe this *was* a perfect fit for me. After all, I'd had nineteen years of business experience, much of it with pharmaceutical companies, followed by thirteen years of nonprofit experience. I knew a lot about fundraising. I had learned much about giving aid to needy families, not to mention having the personal experience of being on the receiving end of medical assistance from abroad.

I agreed to an initial interview for the position and that interview led to several more. Their search was very thorough. Long story short, it was a match all around.

"DON'T WORRY. JUST GO."

I would be taking on bigger responsibilities by accepting the MAP offer, although it would come with a salary cut. I had taken a huge cut in 2001 when I stepped out of the corporate world and my salaries had grown somewhat from there. But this time, my income would fall again. We would have to budget the details of our move carefully.

As I was getting ready to leave ChildFund, my assistant brought out an old Bible that had been in the back of a closet. No one knew where the Bible had come from, but there it was. She handed it to me and I began to flip through it. Only a few passages had been highlighted: the ones in which God tells Moses to advise Joshua, before they go into the Promised Land, *"Be strong and courageous. Do not be afraid or terrified... for the LORD your God goes with you; he will never leave you nor forsake you.... Do not be afraid; do not be discouraged"* (Deuteronomy 31:6, 8 NIV).

That last word was important because I do tend to get discouraged. It was as if God was speaking directly to me, saying, "Steve, don't worry about this move. I am sending you, and I will prepare the way. Don't worry. Just go."

MAP's administrative office is in Atlanta, Georgia, for strategic reasons. There's a large concentration of health-related corporations, research centers, and global nonprofits there, including the CDC. But Atlanta would be an expensive place to live. Sook Hee and I thought that Brunswick, Georgia, where most of the MAP employees and volunteers work in the distribution center, might be a better choice. Brunswick was chosen in 1985 when MAP made the big move from the Chicago area to the East Coast. Since most of the medicines are sent by sea, it helps to have the warehouse and distribution center right on the coast, halfway between the two deep-water ports of Savannah, Georgia, and Jacksonville, Florida, and right off Interstate 95. MAP built a large "green" facility in Brunswick in 2008.

Once we put our Richmond house on the market, it sold relatively quickly. The house we found in Brunswick was priced a little too high at first, but a few percentage points got knocked off. As we were driving from Richmond to Brunswick in September 2014, the bank was wiring the funds from the sale of our Virginia home so we could close on the Brunswick house. Clearly, God was expediting things. Of course, we could trust Him when He said, "Don't worry. Just go."

MAP'S HUMBLE BEGINNINGS

MAP International is a sixty-five-year-old Christian nonprofit that's a very efficient medical relief and disaster response provider. It helps more than ten million people every year get access to life-changing medicines and healthcare supplies with no strings attached, regardless of their faith or religious background. Pharmaceutical companies donate extra medicines, which we then distribute through our partners in needy countries around the world.

MAP had its humble beginnings under the leadership of the late Dr. J. Raymond Knighton. In 1954, he was running the administrative office of the Christian Medical Society (CMS) in Chicago, working in an office so small that it did not even have closet space. A major pharmaceutical company, believing that Dr. Knighton had developed a network to distribute medical supplies to needy countries, decided to donate eleven tons of surplus medicine to CMS—without asking first. Knighton and his secretary had to scramble. He purchased an inexpensive two-wheel hand truck, and for eight hours straight, he personally carted boxes up the small passenger elevator to hastily-arranged storage space. As it happened, a number of medical missionaries were about to come to Chicago for a meeting of the American Medical Association, and he managed to send all of the boxes home with them.

Then, almost before he could get back to his ordinary duties, Knighton got a call regarding the polio epidemic in India; the caller was wondering if he could obtain some of the newly released Salk polio vaccine. This was not part of his job description, but Knighton used his personal contacts in the pharmaceutical industry to arrange for a donation of vaccines from Eli Lilly and even have them specially packed and hand-delivered.

By this time, it was becoming obvious that the Christian Medical Society needed to handle charitable donations and that Ray Knighton should head the effort. The rest is history. Medical Assistance Programs has now been distributing medicines for sixty-five years and counting.

BALANCING INNOVATION WITH HIGH STANDARDS

From the beginning, MAP has always demonstrated an ability to innovate and flex with the times and circumstances, while maintaining impeccable standards of accountability, integrity, impartiality, and service. This has helped it to flourish, with adept leadership as a key component. Governance comes not only from the salaried staff, but also from a well-rounded board of directors drawn from pertinent spheres of expertise.

The job of any managerial leader consists largely of solving problems, and I shouldered the primary responsibility for that at MAP. Starting in 2015, we had to take a hard look at the organization's ongoing financial viability and make some difficult decisions. As part of our strategic planning process to focus MAP on the core mission that we do really well—acquire and dispense medicine and health supplies—we decided to consolidate our efforts. MAP used to maintain a presence in eight other countries, with paid staff and overhead expenses, but we now have transitioned out of country-by-country operations, relying instead on local entities, each of which can be its own boss. This is much more sustainable all around, and it will enable us to expand our distribution into more countries, serving more people with the same resources. Each partner organization provides "boots on the ground" to distribute the medical supplies efficiently.

Over the years, MAP International has earned a reputation for being a proficient organization that delivers high-quality medicines and medical supplies to needy people with remarkably low overhead. This is a reputation I intend to maintain!

THE DRIVE TO ERADICATE POLIO

What does it take to eradicate a global disease? A lot of dedicated people, time, and money. In the case of polio, as with the now-eradicated disease of smallpox, it takes an effective, inexpensive, and easily-administered vaccine as well.

When the first safe and effective polio vaccine was released in 1955, it was hailed as a miracle drug. That year alone, polio had infected 13,850 people, killing 1,043 of them, and everyone was afraid. Even in the 1980s, after vaccinations had eliminated polio in developed countries, a thousand new cases were diagnosed each day in the rest of the world.

How different my own life would have been if I had been vaccinated as a baby! But the timeline of my life overlaps the timeline for the development and release of the polio vaccine. There is simply no way that this American miracle could have made its way to post-war Korea in time to prevent me from getting polio.

Much has changed in my lifetime. For over a quarter of a century, a powerful coalition has been doing everything in their power to make polio a thing of the past by administering the vaccine to everyone they can reach. Launched in 1988, the Global Polio Eradication Initiative

(GPEI) consists of governments and health organizations working with local healthcare providers and countless volunteers. Its partners include the World Health Organization (WHO), Rotary International, the U.S. Centers for Disease Control and Prevention (CDC), the United Nations Children's Fund (UNICEF), and the Bill & Melinda Gates Foundation.[14] Dr. Bill Foege's methods for eradicating smallpox are being used to maximum advantage to help to eradicate polio.

According to WHO, this initiative is the largest internationally coordinated public health effort in history. In the past twenty years, more than 20 million volunteers worldwide have collectively immunized nearly 3 billion children.

Rotary International has been working to eliminate poliomyelitis around the world for more than thirty years. In 1985, they launched their PolioPlus polio eradication program, the first-ever initiative to tackle the polio problem through the mass vaccination of children. Rotary has contributed more than $1.7 billion and countless volunteer hours, while the organization's advocacy efforts have led to $7.2 billion in contributions for the effort from donor governments. I'm humbled to be a part of the global effort to eradicate polio as a member of the Atlanta Rotary Club.

In 1979, Rotary's first project, to immunize children in the Philippines, led to many other international trips, one of which I was privileged to serve on—a polio-immunization outreach to the slums of New Delhi, India, in 2017. In India, children whose legs have been paralyzed are called "crawlers" because that's how they get around. Sook Hee went with me. I am an active Rotarian and I also represent MAP wherever I go. Yet in India, as a polio survivor myself, someone with

14. See Bill Gates' article, "The Best Investment I've Ever Made," *The Wall Street Journal*, January 16, 2019, archived at https://www.wsj.com/articles/bill-gates-the-best-investment-ive-ever-made-11547683309.

visible disabilities, I could be even more persuasive in presenting the case to mothers and children.

I told them, "Look at my legs. Polio did that. I did not have a chance to get immunized. Don't miss your chance today."

At this writing, four regions of the world have been certified polio-free—North and South America, Europe, Southeast Asia, and the Western Pacific. People are still contracting and transmitting the polio virus in Afghanistan, Pakistan, Nigeria, Niger, and Indonesia.[15] Until polio is eradicated, as smallpox was, efforts must continue despite the challenges of cultural restrictions, insufficient public infrastructure, geographic isolation, and even armed conflict.

We cannot afford to relax our efforts as long as any viable virus remains in any part of the human population. With worldwide air travel being what it is, someone could carry the polio virus from a struggling country and infect vulnerable people in a polio-free country who have not received the vaccine. Even children in the United States are not safe until the world has seen its last case of polio. According to Rotary International, if all eradication efforts stopped today, within ten years, polio could paralyze as many as 200,000 children each year.

Besides eradication efforts, we cannot forget the people who, like me, contracted the virus and suffer lifelong complications as a result. While MAP is not working directly on the polio eradication effort, we are supporting the global initiative through ongoing medical care. This CEO on crutches may be one of the best advertisements for early medical intervention.

---

15. For detailed information on the initiative, visit http://polioeradication.org.

VACCINATIONS ARE VITAL

It should go without saying that I believe in vaccinations. When Sook Hee and I went with Rotary International to India, we took along a reporter, Ariel Hart from the *Atlanta Journal-Constitution,* who wrote an article about our trip. Here is an excerpt about our visit to India's only hospital polio ward:

> Two days into Steve's mission in India, he learns that parents in two Indian states are resisting the nation's next step in vaccinations, measles, because of rumors they've read on the internet that the vaccine causes autism. The disgraced scientist who popularized the idea had his paper repudiated by the journal that published it, but the rumor persists in some circles.
>
> The news affronts Steve.
>
> "The parent has all the power," he says. "If they decide not to get the child vaccinated because of something they believe, it's the child that gets sick and lives the rest of their life with the consequences."
>
> Steve comes face-to-face with those consequences one day at St. Stephen's Hospital in Delhi...[where] young men handicapped by polio will spend months undergoing surgeries and physical rehabilitation in hopes that they will transition from crawling to walking with braces....
>
> Dressed in his corporate shirt and slacks and with his head held high, Steve...projects power and success to the patients. A translator relays the story he tells of his life, and his listeners are rapt. Their eyes glance down to his crutches when they get to the part about him being a CEO.
>
> "We can't use our bodies," Steve tells them. "But we can use our brains."

> …They want to know if he is married, if he has children, if the children have jobs of their own. He tells them about his son and daughter and their careers. He points out Sook Hee standing at the side of the room, smiling.[16]

The anti-vaccination movement is in the news these days, and yes, I find it disturbing. I know that if children are not protected from a disease they can be vaccinated against, they have the potential to contract it and spread it. It could become a life sentence, as it did for me.

The anti-vaccination movement argues that the risks of vaccination are too great, but most medical professionals would argue the opposite. Take measles, for example. Here is an excerpt from an educational resource published by the College of Physicians of Philadelphia:

> The risks of natural infection outweigh the risks of immunization for every recommended vaccine. For example, wild measles infection causes encephalitis (inflammation of the brain) for one in 1,000 infected individuals. Overall, measles infection kills two of every 1,000 infected individuals. In contrast, the combination MMR (measles, mumps and rubella) vaccine results in a severe allergic reaction only once in every million vaccinated individuals, while preventing measles infection. The benefits of vaccine-acquired immunity extraordinarily outweigh the serious risks of natural infection.[17]

I think it's our responsibility to take the small risks for the sake of the much greater good.

---

16. Ariel Hart, "Driven to Succeed: Steve Stirling's commitment to eradicate polio is personal," *The Atlanta Journal-Constitution*, June 11, 2017 (http://specials.myajc.com/stirling).
17. See "Do Vaccines Cause Autism?," "Top 20 Questions About Vaccination," and other articles from the College of Physicians of Philadelphia at https://www.historyofvaccines.org.

Too much of the so-called "research" out there is outdated or fear-mongering. Even after they find out that the vaccine-autism connection was false and the research has been invalidated, people still believe the false information that vaccines cause autism. We need to learn how to get information from reliable sources. Just because information is "out there," published and republished, does not mean it's true! Please, if you care about your kids' welfare, get them vaccinated!

ALWAYS REACHING OUT

Sometimes, people ask me, "Would you rather not have had polio?" Of course, I would rather not have had it! Who would want it? But I'm glad God allowed me to get polio for a purpose. I believe I was "saved to serve"—rescued by Him and positioned to represent the Lord to people who can receive what I have to offer because I speak from first-person experience. I intend to keep reaching out to others as long as I have breath.

It's advantageous for me to be a Korean-American adoptee who had polio and experienced the downside of life in a developing country like Korea was in the 1950s. I was forced to deal with the overt discrimination against people with disabilities, such as the idea that you are being punished by God, or your parents did something wrong. When I reach out, people listen to me. Whether I am dispensing medicines in a Third World country or speaking about God at a Christian conference, I do not come across as a privileged American. I am privileged only in that polio has been one of the crutches of my success. I've leaned on it, overcame it, and I've become stronger for it.

My success in the corporate world was the other crutch. The money it brought me didn't make me happy. It was only when I let go of it and made Jesus my Lord as well as my Savior that I could follow His plan for my life. With Him leading me and listening to His still small voice, I have found true happiness.

Getting older has slowed me down somewhat, especially since shoulders are not meant to be weight-bearing joints for a lifetime on crutches, but I can still travel to other countries, and I can still speak out for MAP and for God. When people ask me, "Are you going to retire?" I can only reply, "Well, we'll have to see what God has planned for us." Sook Hee and I would like to retire someday, but we will never retire from being fruitful in serving our Lord, even in our golden years.

EPILOGUE

Now this I say, he who sows sparingly will also reap sparingly, and he who sows bountifully will also reap bountifully. Each one must do just as he has purposed in his heart, not grudgingly or under compulsion, for God loves a cheerful giver. And God is able to make all grace abound to you, so that always having all sufficiency in everything, you may have an abundance for every good deed.
—2 Corinthians 9:6–8 (NASB)

When Christians talk about "divine appointments," they are usually referring to circumstances, most often interpersonal, that are more than happy coincidences because they have been orchestrated by God. I have learned to pray for these...and to expect them.

One Sunday morning, I was in an airport because I had to be someplace by Monday. I was feeling a little sorry for myself because I was missing church and my family. As I sat by my gate in an overcrowded waiting area, reading a small New Testament, I closed my eyes and breathed a brief prayer: *God, use me today for Your glory.* I opened my eyes and saw a young man from India across the room; he seemed to be walking directly toward me. He stopped in front of me and asked, "Sir, do you have the time?" So I told him what time it was and then we started making small talk. He was traveling to California to take a job as a software programmer and he didn't know anybody there. I had a small New Testament with me, and I used it to start sharing the gospel with him. By the time we got on the airplane, I asked him, "Would you like to pray and receive Jesus Christ as your Lord and Savior?" and he said yes.

That's just one example. The same sort of thing has happened in taxis and even in saunas. (Sook Hee calls it my "sauna ministry.") When I'm in a health club sauna after a swim, usually with just one other guy, I can start a conversation in a natural way by saying something like, "God gives you one body, and you have to take care of it. When I get to heaven, I'll have a new body. I'm looking forward to that. I won't have crutches anymore. I know for sure that I'm going to heaven."

Most of them ask me, "How do you know for sure?" Then I share the gospel with them and, on numerous occasions, they pray to receive Jesus as their Lord and Savior, right there sweating in the sauna. (Sometimes I can end with a joke: "It's going to be a lot hotter in hell than it is right now in this sauna!")

I once met a Middle Eastern guy in a sauna in Federal Way, Washington. Months later, I was in Indianapolis for a meeting and afterward, I went out to get a cab. The driver was the same guy I had shared the gospel with in that sauna! He also remembered that occasion, so we continued our conversation.

Such encounters are not always successful, but I know they are divinely appointed.

Looking back on my life, I can now see God's hand on everything, even the fiascos. I have complete faith that He will complete what He has begun with me, as Scripture tells us:

"I am sure that God who began the good work within you will keep right on helping you grow in his grace until his task within you is finally finished on that day when Jesus Christ returns."

(Philippians 1:6 TLB)

"We know that all that happens to us is working for our good if we love God and are fitting into his plans." (Romans 8:28 TLB)

And while my own life circumstances are truly unique, I firmly believe that everyone who calls on the name of the Lord Jesus as Savior, and goes on to make Him Master and Lord, will finish up with every page of his or her divine appointment book filled in. God is the Ruler of the universe, down to the smallest detail, and throughout human history, He has enlisted people like you and me as full participants in the activities of His kingdom. It's all for His glory, and He spares no effort in directing our steps toward the particular goal He has chosen for us.

Can you see His hand in your own life? Your story will not be like mine, but both of our stories have the same Author. God has saved you for a purpose, whether or not you can identify it in so many words. It took me half of my life to figure it out, but now I know that He saved me so I could help needy children and families around the world. My particular set of disabilities and disadvantages was *good* after all. I'm not bitter because I know that God is using everything for His glory. I look forward to being with Him in heaven, but in the meantime, if I can share His love with people or prevent one more child from suffering, I will.

I am passionate about what I do with MAP International, with Rotary's polio eradication campaign, and with sharing the gospel. He is keeping me busy, and I wouldn't have it any other way. As long as I remain on earth, I want to continue to work in these harvest fields where God has placed me, *"making the most of every opportunity"* (Ephesians 5:16 NIV).

I want to pay close attention to His directions and corrections because I belong to *Him* now.

I don't do this work alone. I'm totally dependent on God. And while Sook Hee describes herself as my shadow, supporting me from behind, I know that sometimes, shadows are in front of us when the sunlight shines at the right angle. For most of my adult life, God has accomplished His will for my life primarily through the tireless and unwavering support of my best half, Sook Hee. For this, I am truly grateful.

In heaven, I will not need crutches anymore; I will be whole. So will you, if you have made Jesus your Savior. The important things in life are faith, hope, and love, not accomplishments, appearances, or awards.

Every single one of us is an orphan until the Father adopts us into His eternal family. To God be all the glory!

ABOUT MAP AND ITS PARTNERS

MAP International's mission is to bring health and hope to the world. We are guided by three pillars of service:

- *In disease, health.* MAP provides life-changing medicines and health supplies to those in need around the world.
- *In disaster, hope.* MAP responds to catastrophes around the world, both natural and man-made.
- *In despair, humanity.* MAP serves all people, regardless of religion, gender, race, nationality, or ethnic background.

Where disease is endemic, MAP works with partners to restore health by providing basic medicines and health supplies where there is little or no access for those living in poverty. Basic medicine is lacking in so many places. The number one killers of small children are diarrhea and upper respiratory infections, both of which are preventable and treatable with antibiotics and oral rehydration solutions. By the same reasoning, we accept donations of basic analgesics and first aid supplies such as tape, gauze, syringes, needles, creams, and ointments—supplies that get used routinely by clinics and hospitals. We also supply a whole range of life-saving prescription medicines that treat common conditions such as diabetes, hypertension, and cardiovascular disease as well as epilepsy and psychiatric illnesses.

By sending medicine to those in need, our assistance leads to more than improved healthcare because a healthier population means stronger families and communities. In developing countries, the average lifespan is only about forty-five to fifty years. This is due in part to hygiene and safety deficiencies, but is more attributable to the poor quality of healthcare.

Assisted by our partners on the ground, MAP gives out free medicines to those who need them the most, helping to break the cycle of poverty.

Even when people *can* afford medicines or health supplies, they may not be able to obtain these, so MAP provides them. People living on less than two dollars a day cannot afford to purchase medicine, and sometimes what they can buy turns out to be counterfeit. At one time, I visited a trauma hospital in Haiti that was staffed by twin brothers from France who are surgeons. They said, "MAP medicine is worth more than gold because even if you could sell the gold, there's no medicine to buy here." In Haiti, healthcare workers have actually gone on strike, not for more money but for medicine.

In 2018, MAP helped 13.6 million people in 104 countries by providing medicines and supplies.

Here are some highlights of MAP's disaster response efforts, which began in 1963, when the organization sent aid to typhoon-stricken Taiwan:

- 1989 – Sent $1.6 million in medicines to assist civilian casualties of the civil war in Panama
- 1999 – Sent $33 million in medicines to Kosovar refugees
- 2001 – After the fall of the Taliban, we airlifted medical supplies to the people of Afghanistan
- 2005 – Aided tsunami-stricken Indonesia and Sri Lanka
- 2006 – Launched mobile health clinics to reach people hit by Hurricanes Katrina and Rita in Louisiana and Mississippi
- 2010 – Collaborated with Love a Child, Harvard University, and others to distribute $20 million in aid after an earthquake leveled the capital of Haiti
- 2014 – Mobilized a special response to the deadly Ebola outbreak in West Africa in the form of 33,000 personal protection suits for healthcare workers along with $18 million in essential medicines and supplies
- 2015 – Sent disaster aid to the cyclone-devastated Pacific island nation of Vanuatu and earthquake survivors in Nepal

In fiscal year 2018, MAP responded to disasters in Guatemala, Bolivia, the Dominican Republic, Kenya, and across the United States. We also sent aid to Syrian refugees in Lebanon and Armenia. When Hurricane Michael hit our own part of the United States in October 2018, MAP was ready with disaster health kits that include antiseptic wipes, soap, toothbrushes, toothpaste, and other critical relief supplies to treat injuries and prevent the spread of illness. Altogether, MAP shipped out 3,327 pallets of supplies weighing more than 940 tons in 2018.

After Hurricanes Irma and Maria devastated Puerto Rico and neighboring islands in September 2017, MAP's considerable response, which continued for almost a year, included fifty-three shipments valued at $8.2 million. These shipments went out to at least seventeen partner organizations in small custom orders, twenty- and forty-foot containers, cargo planes, and two private donor-chartered planes. We sent everything from medicines and health supplies to water filters, leveraging our relationships on the ground with existing MAP partners such as Convoy of Hope.

Wherever despair threatens to overcome people, MAP's extensive network of partners provides medicines and health supplies to help those living in the darkest of conditions. The World Health Organization estimates that as many as two billion people worldwide lack access to life-saving medicines and medical care. As MAP reaches out to more places and partners, we hope to reach exponentially more people with these life-changing remedies.

MAP'S OPERATIONS

MAP International has approximately forty-five employees in Brunswick and Atlanta, Georgia, and scattered across the U.S. As medicines and supplies are received, everything is inventoried by trained employees and shelved efficiently in our 40,000-square-foot distribution center.

This distribution center is also a foreign trade zone where we securely hold the medicines we have procured internationally before we put them into containers for shipment. We partner with U.S. Customs to exceed all standards and regulations.

We could also not accomplish everything that we do without the help of our amazing volunteers. About one hundred regular volunteers from the local community assist us as products are received from pharmaceutical companies and other corporate donors. They prepare all of our prepackaged boxes. In fiscal year 2018, our volunteers logged more than 4,100 hours!

A HUB FOR GLOBAL HEALTH

Atlanta has become the center for global health because more health-related institutions and organizations have headquarters there than any other city in the world. Besides the CDC and MAP, it's home to Emory University and Emory Healthcare, The Carter Center, the Task Force for Global Health, the Cooperative for Assistance and Relief Everywhere (CARE), and MedShare. Atlanta is also the global hub for Delta Air Lines and United Parcel Service, which connect the city with the rest of the world.

Having so many health-related entities in the same place creates a mutually beneficial situation. By working together, each group can contribute what they do best and accomplish much more than they could alone.

HONORING NOTABLE CONTRIBUTIONS

In 2017, MAP established the Bill Foege Global Health Awards to present annually to those individuals who have made especially notable contributions to worldwide health. The award is named for Atlanta epidemiologist Dr. Bill Foege, Emory University's Emeritus Presidential Distinguished Professor of International Health and a Senior Fellow for Global Health at the Bill & Melinda Gates Foundation. He headed the CDC from 1977 to 1983 and has served in a number of leadership positions for organizations such as The Carter Center, founded by former President Jimmy Carter and his wife Rosalynn, and the Task Force for Global Health, the second-largest health-related charity in the world.

Dr. Foege is best known as the head of the successful CDC Smallpox Eradication Program, which claimed final victory over the global scourge of smallpox in 1977. As a result, he is credited for saving more lives than anyone in history. (Three hundred million people died during the twentieth century alone before this horrific disease was eradicated.)

The first Bill Foege Global Health Awards were presented to Rotary International and the Bill & Melinda Gates Foundation because of their extraordinary efforts to eradicate polio.

In 2018, the second annual Bill Foege Global Health Awards went to President Carter and his wife in recognition of their outstanding efforts toward the eradication of neglected tropical diseases, such as Guinea-worm disease, as well as Mrs. Carter's work on behalf of mental health in Liberia. (MAP provides much-needed neuropsychiatric medications that are administered by 230 mental health workers trained by The Carter Center, while MedShare provided medical equipment such as hospital beds and X-ray machines.) It was my honor not only to present the actual award, but to host the Carters at the MAP distribution center in Brunswick.

In 2019, the Carters are the honorary co-chairs of the award presentation in Atlanta.

GIVING TO MAP

To support MAP's mission, please visit www.map.org/ways-to-give. Contributions may also be mailed to: MAP International, 4700 Glynco Parkway, Brunswick, GA 31525.

ABOUT THE AUTHOR

Steve Stirling is president and CEO of MAP International, a faith-based nonprofit providing essential medicines for mission clinics and hospitals in developing countries around the world. Since 1954, MAP has served hundreds of millions of people with medicines and medical supplies through the help of partners, donors, mission hospitals, clinics, and medical mission teams.

Steve earned his B.S. degree in agricultural economics at Cornell University and his MBA in marketing and finance at Northwestern University's Kellogg School of Management. He held marketing positions at several corporations for more than two decades, including Johnson & Johnson, Bristol Meyers Squibb, Con-Agra Foods, and Ameritrade. Steve moved over to the nonprofit sector in June 2001, when he became vice president of marketing operations for World Vision.

Steve and his wife, Sook Hee, make their home in Brunswick, Georgia. They have two grown children, Richard, a lawyer, and Racheal, a copywriter.